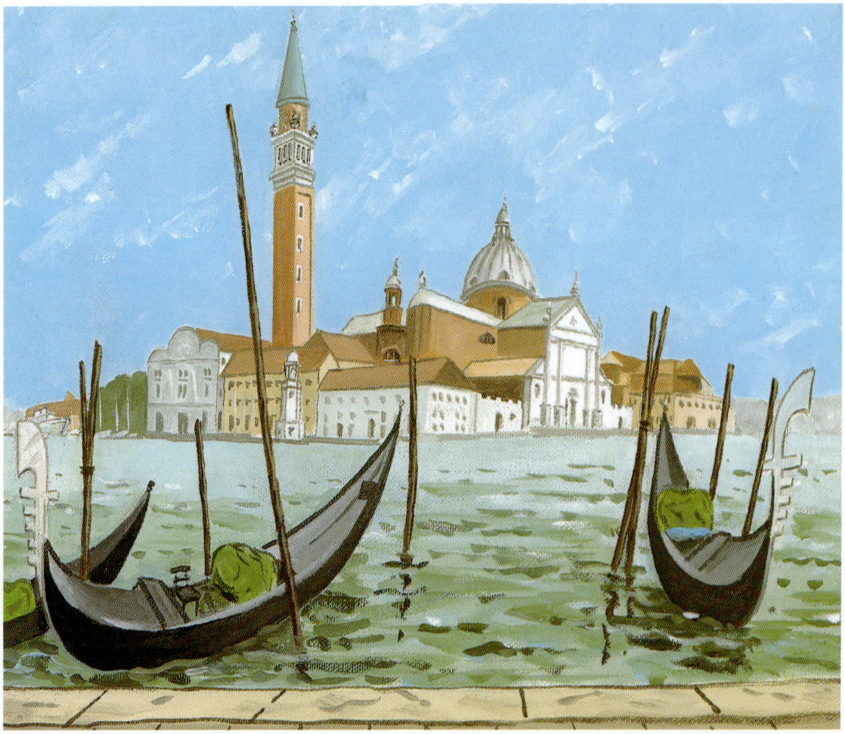

OIL PAINTING

STYLES AND TECHNIQUES

This edition published in 2013
By SpiceBox™
12171 Horseshoe Way
Richmond, BC
Canada V7A 4V4

First published in 2009

ISBN 10: 1-77132-046-X
ISBN 13: 978-1-77132-046-7

CEO and Publisher: Ben Lotfi
Creative Director: Garett Chan
Art Director: Christine Covert
Production: James Badger & Mell D'Clute
Sourcing: Janny Lam
Photography: Peter Raymond, Southport.
Origination by DL Repro Ltd., London EC
1 M 4DD

For more SpiceBox products and information, visit our website:
www.spiceboxbooks.com

Manufactured in China

3 5 7 9 10 8 6 4 2

CONTENTS

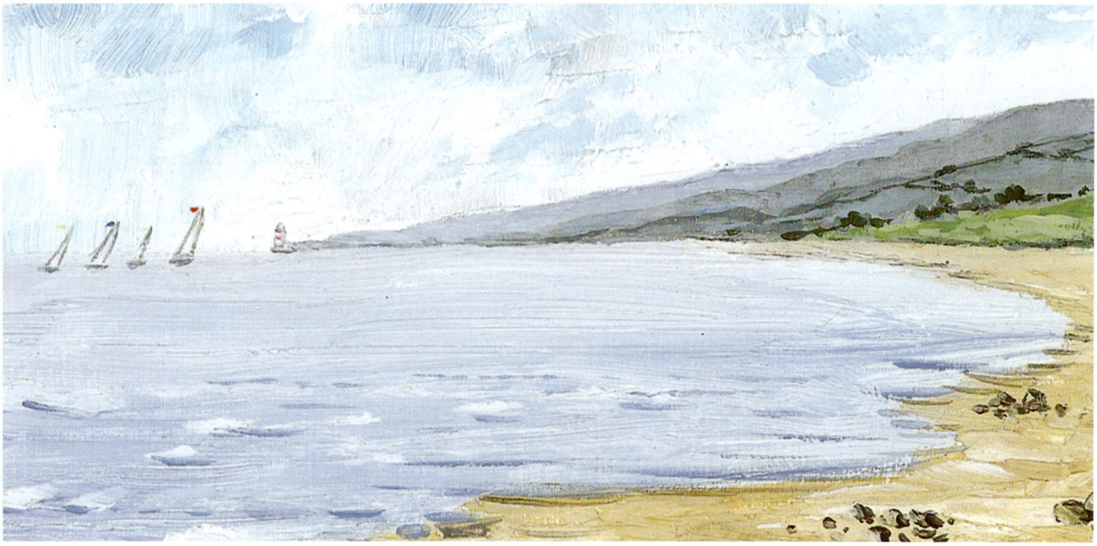

ABOUT THE AUTHOR: PHILIP BERRILL, THE FLYING ARTIST

Philip Berrill is a professional artist, tutor, lecturer and author—his method of learning to paint taught and enjoyed worldwide. Born in 1945 in Northampton, England, Philip now lives in Southport with his wife Sylvia and daughter Penelope.

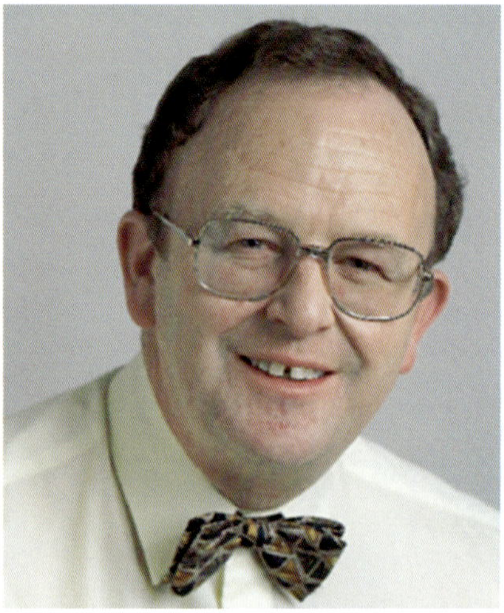

Author, artist, lecturer, Philip Berrill

Philip recalls how he discovered paint at age three. It was a sunny afternoon, he wandered into his father's greenhouse and saw at the far end of the building a large bucket of whitewash and a tubular pump sprayer. Philip loaded the sprayer and had a lovely afternoon covering all of his father's best tomatoes and plants with white. He had discovered paint, and that it could change how you see the world.

At the age of fourteen, Philip decided he would make a living as a professional artist. He came under the influence of the Welsh artist and tutor John Sullivan. Philip held his first solo exhibition at the age of eighteen, followed by other group and one-man exhibitions. At the age of twenty-eight, Liverpool University held a major exhibition of his work—the direct result of which was that Philip could realize his ambition to become a professional artist. He launched very successful art classes using his unique approach to teaching, sketching and painting. These classes proved so popular Philip went on to develop worldwide correspondence courses. In the 1980s, he embarked on the next stage of his career, which led to his being nicknamed "*The Flying Artist*." After offering sought-after painting vacation courses in Great Britain, he organized additional painting holiday retreats in Europe—in Rome, Venice, Florence and Paris. Subsequently Philip lectured and demonstrated painting in America and the Middle East. Philip's much-admired exhibition, *The Italian Connection*, consists of sketches and paintings from his Italian journeys, and other European locations. Philip's love and enthusiasm for sketching and painting is infectious. He believes that art should be for everyone, and that you are never too young or too old to begin sketching. His students have ranged from ten to eighty, and he continues to enjoy passing on his enthusiasm and knowledge, gained over thirty years, to people from all walks of life.

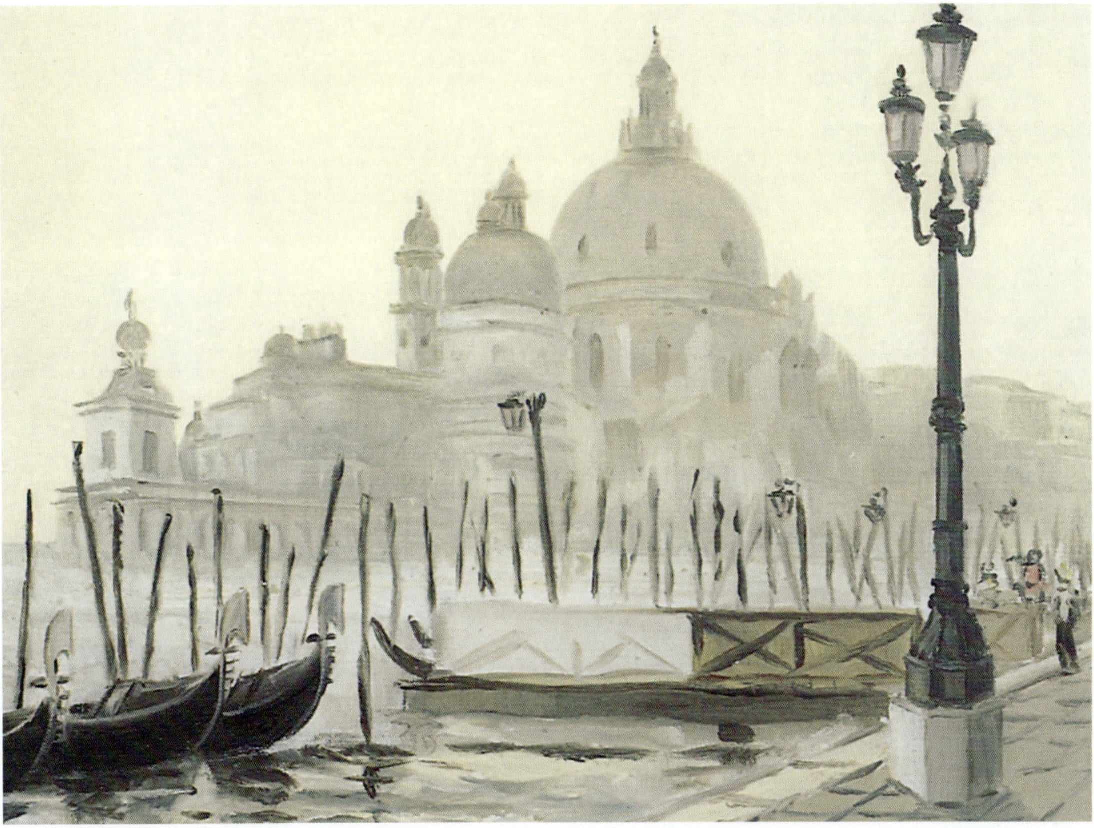

Basilica di Santa Maria della Salute

Philip has designed his method for people of all ages and all abilities, and over recent years has produced a series of art videos. These videos led to an invitation to produce and present a thirteen-part television series, *Paint with the Flying Artist,* and that project in turn led to the writing and illustration of this series of art books designed especially for you. These books cover a wide range of mediums, techniques and subjects—to introduce you to the joy and pleasure of sketching and painting. These beautifully presented books come with all the materials you will need to get started painting and drawing. The compact form and portability of the kit allows freedom and spontaneity to capture each moment of inspiration that Philip demonstrates in his own work. The hope is that these books will assist you in your own journey of sketching and painting.

INTRODUCTION

I fell in love with oil painting at the age of thirteen. One day, I went into my art teacher's storeroom and met for the first time the rich, wonderful, aromatic smell of oil paints. The storeroom was in darkness. I switched on the light. There before me, in neat boxes, were row upon row of brand new, untouched oil paints, rows of oil painting brushes; new, unused canvases; painting boards; and bottles of a liquid named linseed oil, and turpentine, to mix with the paint. When I opened the boxes, the orderly tubes of oil paint looked enticing, and seemed to wait for squeezing onto the artist's palette. The range of color was completely dazzling—oil paint captivated my senses, it was love at first sight.

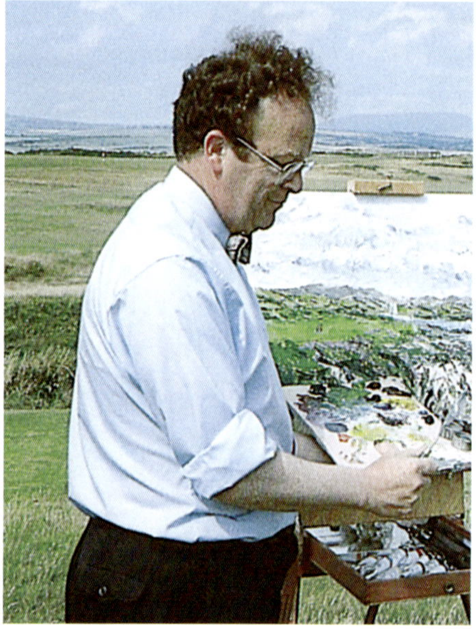

Philip Berrill at work in plein air

I begged my art tutor, John Sullivan, to tell me all about how to use oil paints and to let me try them. He did, and I discovered the joy and picture-making possibilities of these paints. To this day, my fingers still tingle with excitement as I set my oil paints ready to put brush and paint to canvas. Oil paint is user-friendly. One can achieve great richness and depth of color and tone in the medium. Oil paint can be applied opaquely with stiff hogs hair brushes, or stiff synthetic hair which imparts an interesting texture to each brush stroke. Oil paint works with smoother sable, or soft synthetic hair brushes for a brushmark-free, smooth finish. A painting or palette knife can apply a highly textured paint layer known as *impasto*.

Oil paints offer great freedom to both the newcomer to painting and the more experienced painter. You can paint highly detailed pictures, looser or more impressionistic pictures, or you can create bold, free-flowing pictures with just a few sweeping strokes of a brush. You can modify oil paint pictures while working on the painting, or after letting it dry. If the paint is still wet, mistakes scrape off with a palette knife and a little care, or wipe away with a clean, dry cloth. If the paint is dry, an area can be overpainted, as oil paint is opaque. Oil paintings can be produced by the technique known as *alla prima*; that is, wet paint on wet paint. Or can be built up in stages, layer by layer, allowing each layer to dry, or become touch-dry, before the next layer is applied.

The aim of this book is to give you a sound understanding of the medium and techniques, so that you can use them to create your own paintings in your own style. If you are a beginner, what joys you have to come. If you already paint, I would like to think I can help you develop your talent and skills further.

The Origins of Oil Painting

The Fifteenth Century Netherlandish brothers Van Eyck traditionally receive credit for the discovery of oil painting. However, it is now widely understood that oil painting evolved from prior times. Early works on the art and technique of painting give recipes for cooked, sun-bleached and drying oils. Cennino Cennini's *Il Libro dell'Arte,* or Craftsman's Handbook, is an enlightening guide to the methods and techniques of the Renaissance period. Northern European artists used oils with pigment before the southern European artists, and by the sixteenth century, most easel painting used oil paint. Before that, paintings were either frescos, painted onto the wet or dry plaster of walls, or egg tempera paintings done on a wooden surface, or panel. The use of primed canvas stretched on a wooden frame meant that a large painting could move about. When dry, the canvas could be unpinned from the stretcher, and the wooden stretcher frame collapsed—the painting taken from the studio, to the customer, and re-assembled at its final location. The convenience of a superb range of artist's materials, including paints, brushes and canvases means that today we can concentrate on the art of painting pictures.

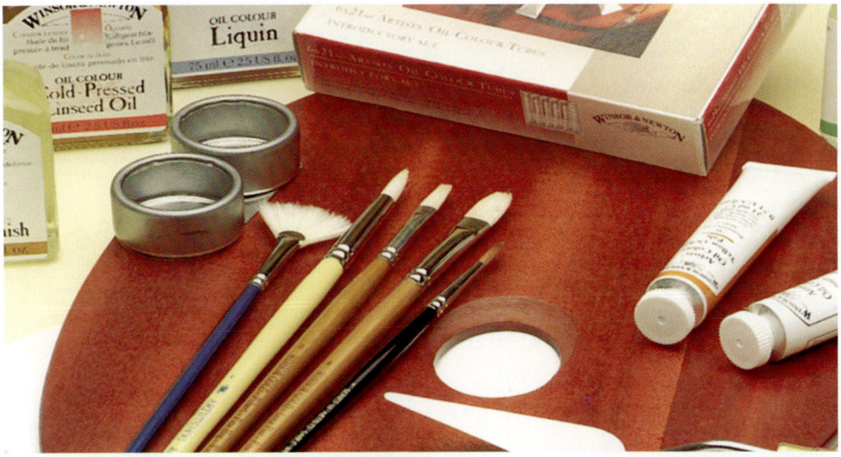

Some tools of the painter's trade

MATERIALS FOR OIL PAINTING

Oil Paint

Oil paints derive from combining pigment with drying, or semi-drying, oil. The paint, with exposure to the air, oxidizes and creates an elastic skin that gradually hardens on the surface of the canvas or painting surface. Cold-pressed linseed oil, poppy oil, safflower oil and soya oil are the most commonly used oils in the manufacture of oil paints.

Mediums, Solvents, Dilutants and Varnishes

Distilled Turpentine

Turpentine is colorless. Artists use it to thin the oil paint. The resulting dry paint has a matte finish. The paint is normally touch-dry within two to three days. Distilled turpentine has a very pronounced smell. It is flammable and, like all bottles, should be clearly marked and stored well out of reach of children.

White Spirit or Turpentine Substitute

This is an economical diluent for cleaning brushes. It has a characteristic odor, less pronounced than turpentine. It is flammable and should be stored in the same manner as distilled turpentine.

Sansodor

This is an alternative to the stronger smelling turpentine.

Liquin

Liquin is a popular oil painting medium that increases the flow, or the transparency, of oil paint. It allows for smooth brushwork, subtle blending and the painting of fine detail. It dries quickly, often becoming touch-dry within eighteen hours. I find this a great advantage when building my picture in touch-dry layers, especially when painting on holiday, or on painting expeditions away from the studio.

Varnish

A protective coat of varnish is applied when the paint dries. A coat of gloss varnish will impart the traditional gleam to the painting. A coat of matte varnish, while protecting the picture surface from the atmosphere, reduces or eliminates the reflection of light on the picture's surface. Varnishes come in bottles and apply to the picture surface with a clean varnishing brush. Winsor and Newton produces an ozone-friendly can of Artists' Picture Varnish, a gloss varnish, which many painters find convenient. Detailed instructions on varnishing your painting figure in the chapter headed *Varnishing and Framing*.

Oil Painting Supports

An oil painting support is simply the surface on which you paint. It can be rigid or flexible. Many companies manufacture the supports acrylic-primed and ready to paint. Acrylic-primed supports work for oil painting, acrylic painting, and for use with griffin alkyd paints.

Oil Sketching Paper

This is a stout paper impressed with a canvas-like texture. It comes in single sheets, but commonly appears bound in oil sketching pads. It is ideal for trying out ideas when the permanence of work is not essential, but it can tear or crease. If you paint a study on oil sketching paper that you want to keep, you can glue the picture, when dry, to a sheet of acid-free cardboard.

Oil Painting Boards

Robust cardboard with a sheet of prepared oil sketching paper glued to it provides an inexpensive and practical painting surface. With the availability of good quality, inexpensive cotton canvas, art materials manufacturers have been able to produce and market an economical range of canvas boards. These come in a variety of sizes and have genuine canvas glued to the surface. They are primed and ready for you to paint.

Stretched Canvas

A stretched canvas is a canvas stretched over a special frame and pinned to the sides of the frame to keep the canvas taut. The canvas usually comes primed and ready for painting. It offers the artist a delightful, springy painting surface compared to the rigidity of painting boards. Over a time, a stretched canvas can slacken—regain tension by gently tapping the wedges in the corners of the back.

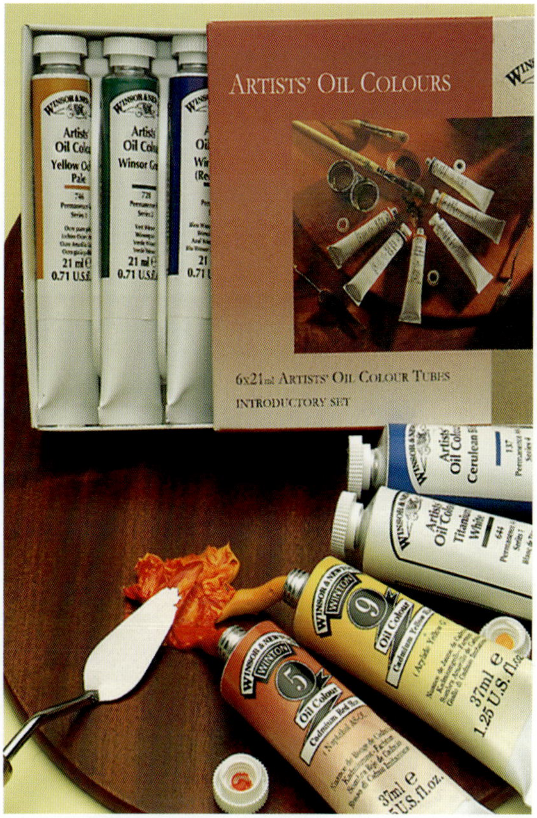

A set of oil paints

BRUSHES

Hog Bristle

The finest bristle brush keeps its shape, retains its working edge and holds a considerable amount of oil paint. It will wear well when used on the coarser surfaces some artists like to use. Bristle is durable, while a little less flexible than sable brushes. Hog bristle brushes come in five main shapes—round, long flat, short flat, fan and filbert. The filbert brush starts flat at the base, but the hair becomes domed at the top. Each shape of brush offers the artist a distinctive brush mark.

Sable

This type of brush provides a very smooth, brush mark-free, finish to your painting, and works well for painting in detail. The precision given by the point of a round sable brush, or the neatness of the edge of a flat sable brush, is of great importance to the artist.

Synthetic Hair Brushes

A type of brush ideally suited to watercolor and water-based paints. While synthetic brushes are available for oil painting, very few match the performance of the traditional oil painting brushes.

Care of Brushes

Wash your brushes using white spirit or turpentine substitute in a jar. Remove surplus turpentine from the brushes using a clean, absorbent cloth. Use cool tap water and household soap to lather the hair of the brushes. When the brushes are clean, rinse them thoroughly. Shake the brushes and reshape the bristles with your fingers. Stand your brushes bristle-end up in a jar to dry.

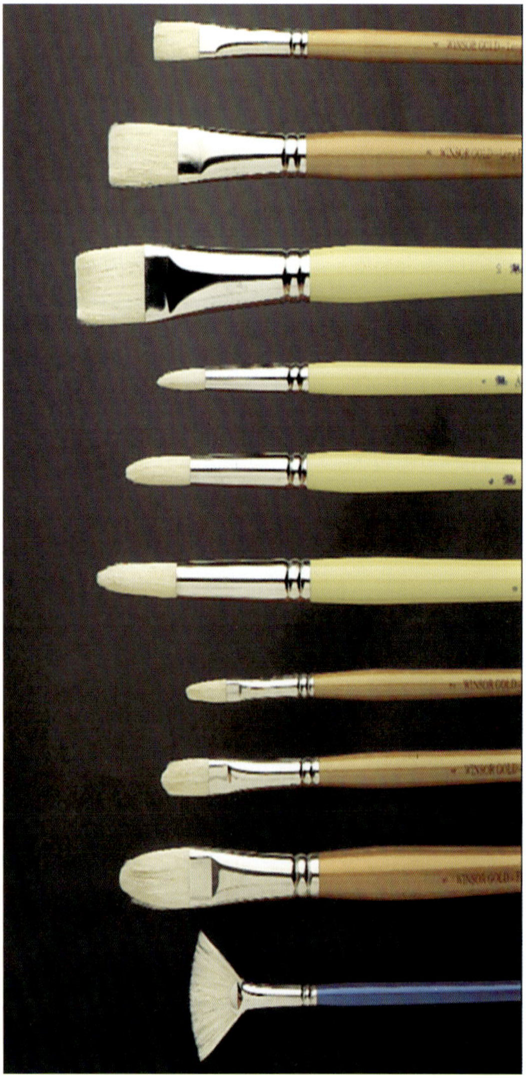

Brushes—the essential tool

PALETTES

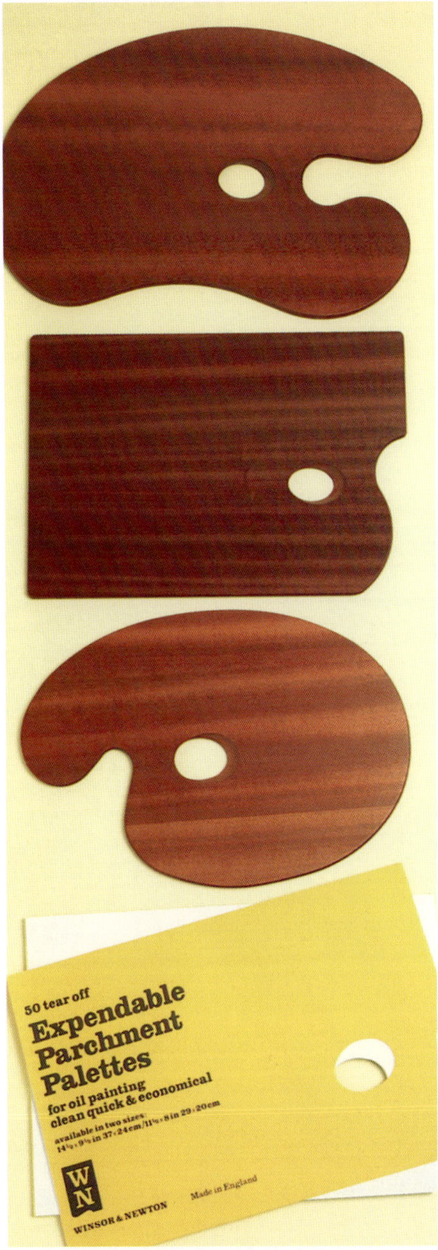

A variety of palettes

Oil paints mix on a palette. Wooden palettes come in oval, rectangular or kidney shapes. The traditional palette is usually mahogany veneered. Birch plywood palettes are a lighter, creamy color. Melamine-faced palettes are white. All need cleaning after use. I recommend the expendable paper palettes. They are clean and economical, and the used pages can be disposed of without mess. They consist of twenty-five to fifty sheets of a special oil-proof paper. They are rectangular in shape and, as with the other palettes, can be held in the hand or laid beside you on a working table.

Dippers

A double metal dipper clips onto the side of your palette. It consists of two metal containers to hold your painting medium and solvent.

Knives

Palette knives are finger-like, moderately flexible steel blades in a wooden handle. They generally mix oil paints together on the palette. A selection of sizes is available. A plastic palette knife is also available.

Painting knifes have a cranked handle to keep the artist's fingers and knuckles away from the painting surface when the painting knife applies oil paint directly to the picture surface. A medium, diamond-shaped painting knife is ideal to begin.

GRIFFIN ALKYD PAINTS

These are very similar to oil paints but manufactured from pigments suspended in an alkyd resin and solvent. The main advantage is the speed with which they dry. I find an area is dry to the touch about eighteen hours later. The range of forty-two colors and the even, buttery consistency make them suitable for all the traditional oil painting techniques. Liquin is the medium used to add to the paint instead of linseed oil or turpentine. Wash brush out and clean exactly as for oil paints.

Oilbars

A new dimension for the artist that offers an exciting new opportunity. Due to their formulation, they are different from oil pastels. A mixture of pigment, linseed oil and special waxes, they enable the artist to draw, work and mix directly on the canvas, without using a brush. Oilbar is available in three sizes.

Sundry Materials

A medium-sized piece of charcoal, some absorbent clean cloth for wiping your brushes, old newspapers to put on your painting table and an overall, smock or old clothes for yourself are all worth collecting. Many people like to keep their art materials neat and tidy in a portable, divided plastic box. It is useful for outdoor painting and for taking your materials to an art class or art club.

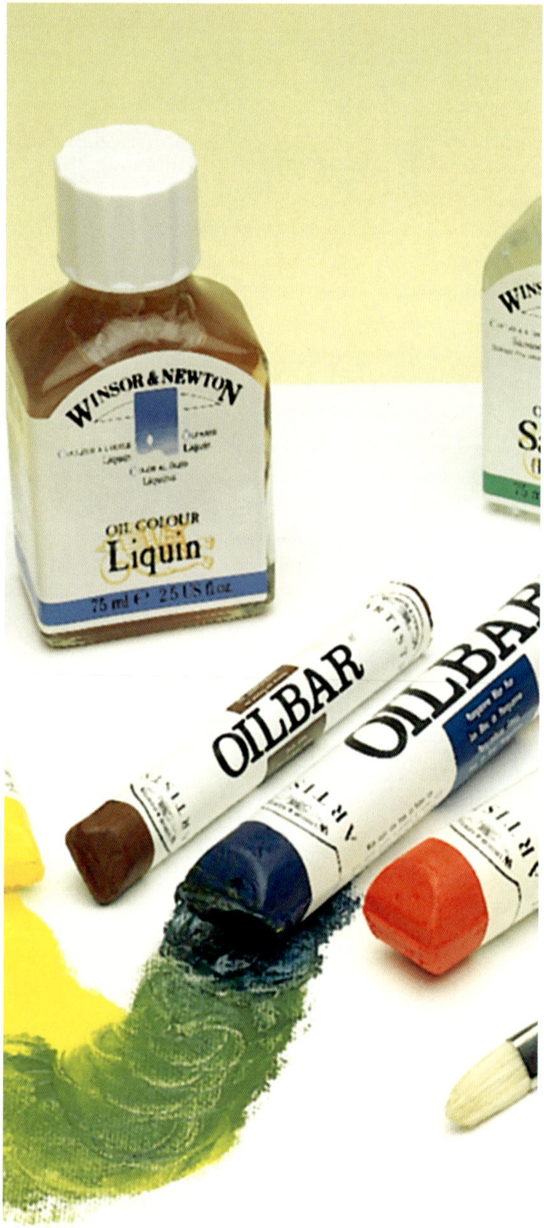

An Assortment of Oil Bars

EASEL

Oil paintings paint best on an easel with the painting vertical, or at an inclined angle. They are especially practical for those artists who like to sit down when painting. Some fold and transport to an art class, art club or other painting location.

In most instances, these can adjust to standing or sitting positions. A table easel, or a lightweight wooden or metal sketching easel makes a practical starting point for newcomers to painting. If space permits, a larger studio easel can be a good investment.

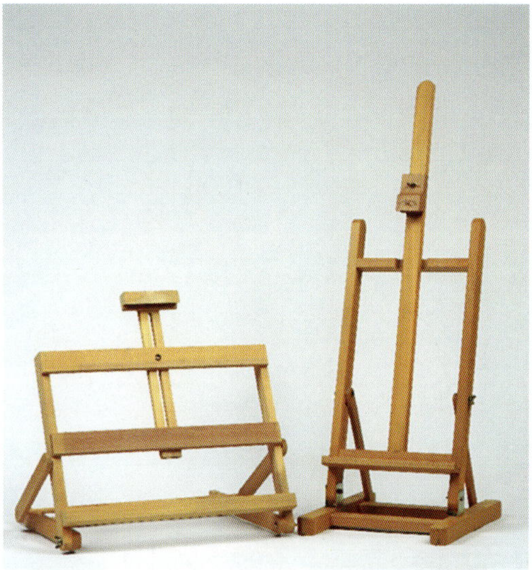

A few varieties of easel

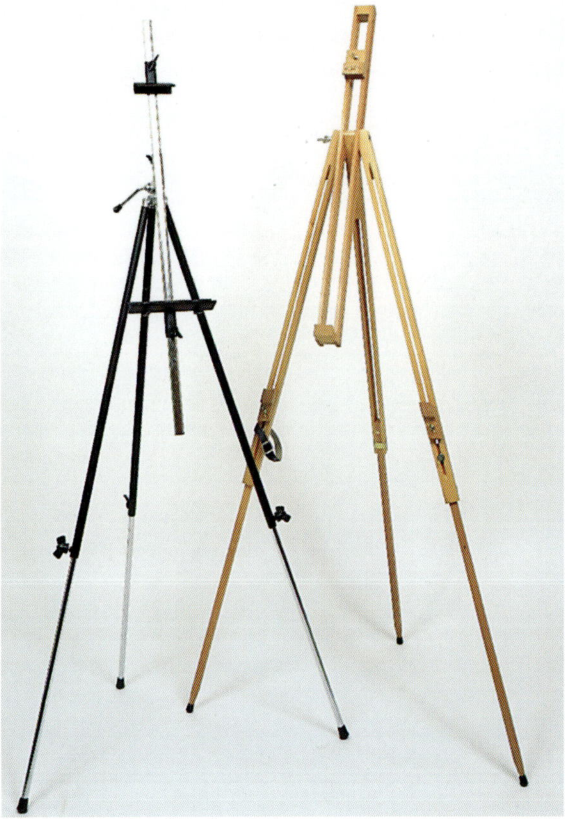

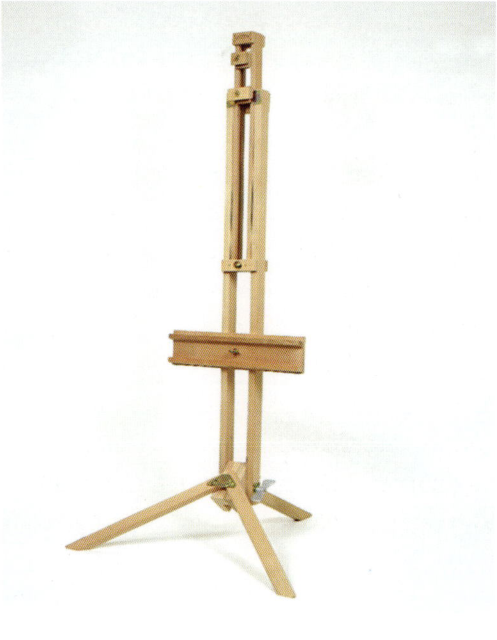

COLOR

Color Mixing

The color charts on these pages are indispensable and are a practical and helpful guide in learning to mix colors.

The first chart shows how the three *Primary Colors*—red, yellow and blue—make the three *Secondary Colors*—orange, mauve and green. The secondary colors can be mixed to make the three *Tertiary Colors*—dark brown, light brown and olive green.

How to Make Black

Three primary colors mixed together produce black. I generally advise people not to use black oil paint to darken a color. It seems to dull and deaden the colors and they lose their clarity.

Complementary Color Wheel

Black is opposite, or complementary, to white. Each color has its opposite color, shown on the *Complemetary Color Wheel*—black/white; yellow/mauve; orange/blue; red/green.

It is a good idea to ask yourself what is the predominant color of your subject and to try to have a splash of the opposite color in the painting. This can have a dramatic effect. If you mix any two opposite or complementary colors together in equal amounts, you produce gray.

Primary Color Chart

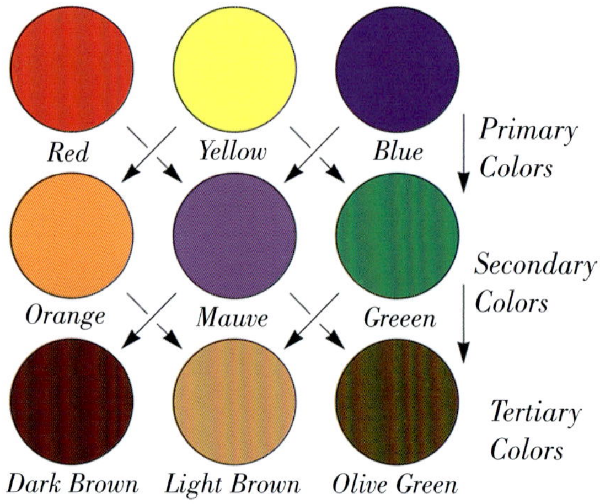

A Complemetary Color Wheel

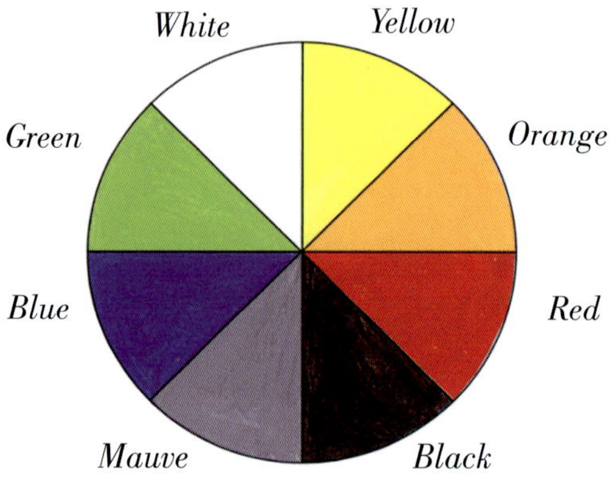

The Color Tint Chart

Group your colors in the way I show. Paint a strong tone of the color in the first of the three boxes then make a medium tone made by adding a little white paint, then a light tone by adding even more white. This will show you the color and two of its lighter shades.

Greens Color Chart

This shows how, with three blues, three yellows, one green and white, you can make twenty-five greens of value to anyone who paints, but especially to the landscape and floral painter. If you paint the charts on paper cut to A4 size, they can be placed in a clear plastic folder to keep them clean when dry, ready for you to refer to when painting.

Color Tint Chart

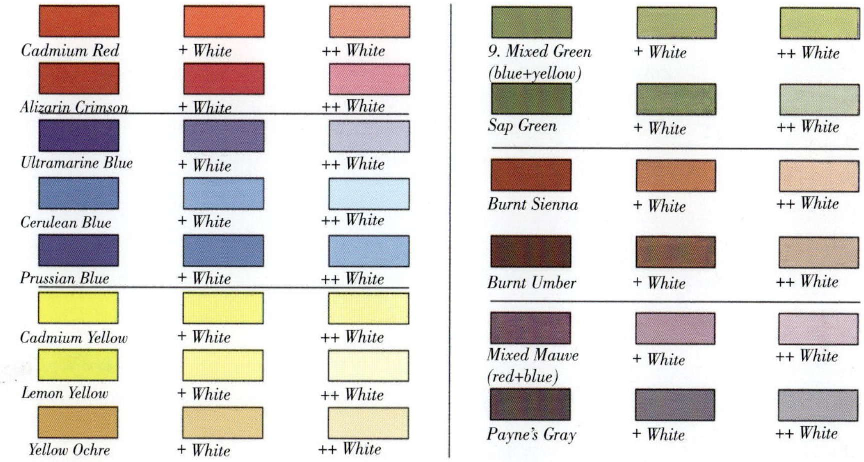

Green Color Chart

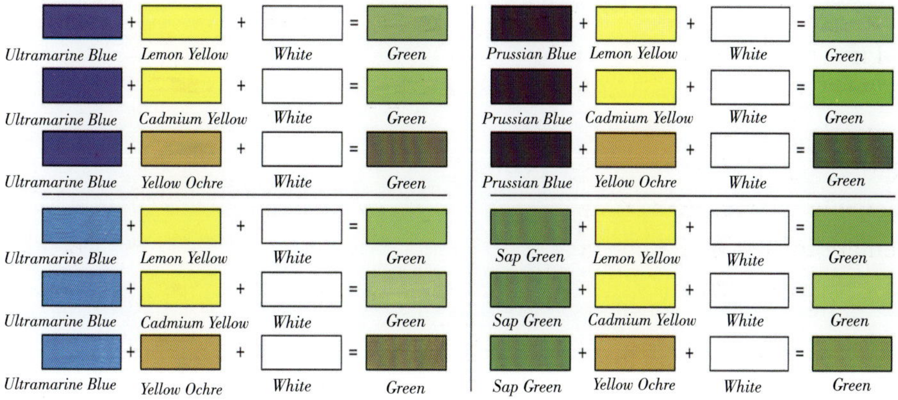

METHODS FOR SKETCHING

I believe in making one or two preliminary sketches of my subject. I do these in my sketchbook, or on some spare pieces of paper, using a 2B pencil. This gives me the chance to examine and explore the subject, and to plan my picture. It is a good habit, and I recommend it to you as a technique to adopt. However, if you are drawing the subject on oil sketching paper, canvas boards or canvas, the pencil lines will dissolve and slightly discolor the paint layer you apply to the picture surface.

The three main methods oil painters use to draw out their subjects on their painting surface are:

Charcoal

1. Use a stick of charcoal and firmly draw out the subject. The line should look black but will easily smudge.

2. Use a clean, dry, soft cloth or duster and vigorously dust the surface of the picture. Remove the loose, smudgy charcoal with a duster, leaving a faint, non-smudging drawing ready to paint.

Fine Paintbrush

Mix a pale gray, or a pale brown, oil paint with turpentine to the consistency of ink. Use a No. 3 or No. 4 round sable or synthetic brush. Sketch the picture onto the painting surface. Because of the amount of turpentine used, the painted lines will dry out quickly. When they dry, you can start painting.

Imprimitura

1. Some artists find the thought of painting onto a clean, unspoilt surface quite daunting, or prefer something other than pure white to work on. They usually make a thin mixture of turpentine and oil paint, often burnt umber. Using a cloth or large brush, they apply the thin color to the painting surface to tint it. The turpentine in the mixture will evaporate in about thirty minutes, leaving a dry surface.

2. Using a darker tone of the same color of oil paint and turpentine, sketch the subject on the tinted background. Various colors work for background tinting. A dull green can make an excellent background for portrait work. Imprimitura is the name for this technique.

Try each method and you will discover the method best suited to you. When you finish your sketch, turn it upside down and look at it before you paint. This handy hint will help identify errors to correct.

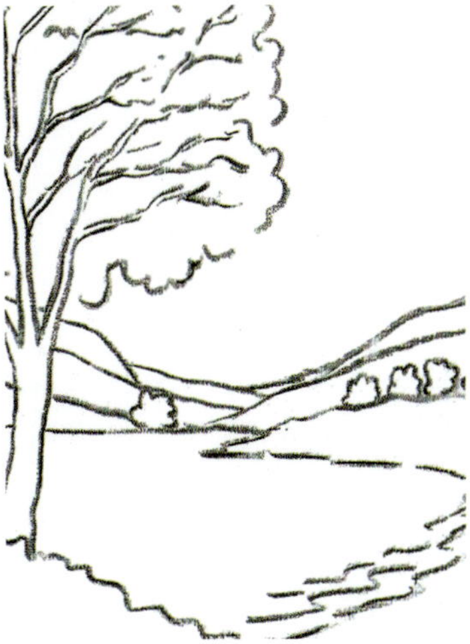

A charcoal sketch before dusting

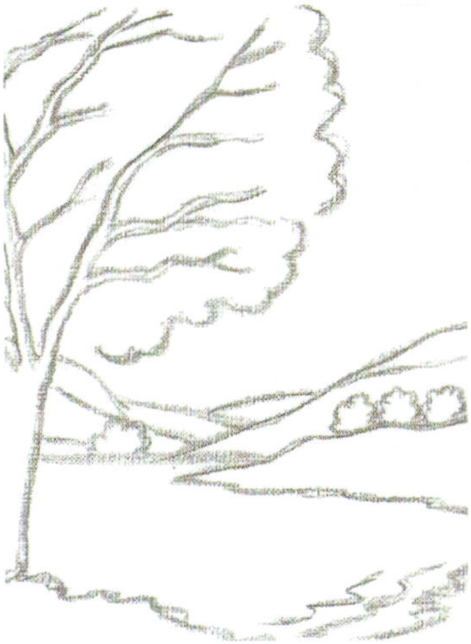

A dusted charcoal sketch

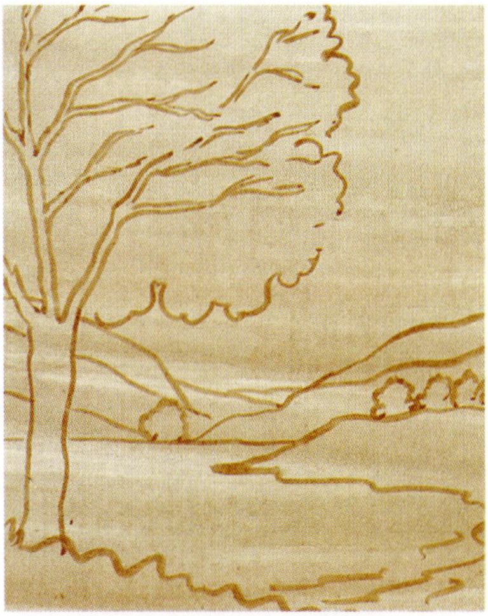

An imprimitura sketch

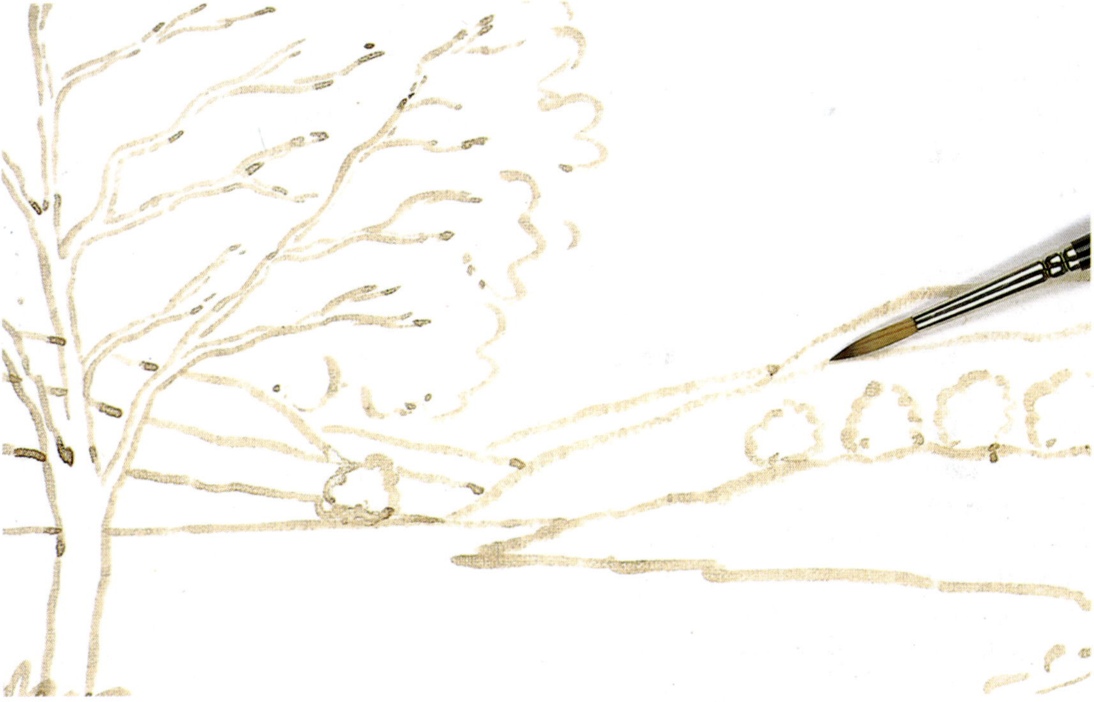

Example of a fine paintbrush sketch

MONOCHROME COFFEE JUG

I always encourage people to try a monochrome painting. Monochrome means one color. Use a single plain-colored item, such as this coffee pot. Painting a monochrome study of it will help you understand how to look for, mix and use the three main tones of light, medium and dark color. It will help you to discover how to look for the darkest features, and the lightest, which play an important role in a successful painting.

1. I suggest that all the demonstration paintings in this book are painted on a support, either oil sketching paper, a canvas board or canvas, measuring 14" x 10" (356 mm x 254 mm), 16" x 12" (406 mm x 305 mm) or 20" x 16" (508 mm x 406 mm). Sketch the coffee pot using the charcoal technique ensuring you dust off the loose charcoal before you start painting.

2. Light Tone. Using turpentine as needed, mix some french ultramarine and white. As the coffee pot is blue, paint a light blue tone, filling in the whole shape of the coffee pot. Use a medium size flat, or filbert, hog bristle paintbrush to apply the paint. Keep the paint thick. You don't want to be able to see the painting surface through the paint.

3. Medium Tone. Add a little more blue to the mixture on your palette. Apply the medium tones shown in the illustration. The light source comes from the left-hand side of the pot, so the shadows, along with the medium and dark tones, will fall to the right-hand side of the coffee pot, away from the light.

4. Dark Tone. Add a little more blue to the mixture on your palette and apply the dark tones. They are to the right of the body of the pot, under the bulbous lower half of the body, spout, and handle, and found on the base and lid.

5. Using very dark blue and a No. 3 round synthetic or sable brush, pick out the darkest features. These are on the lid, spout opening, handle and base of the coffee pot. Likewise, using a very pale, almost white, mixture of blue and white, pick out the highlights on the jug. Add a background and table top in the way shown. This gives a sketchy look to the background to emphasize the jug.

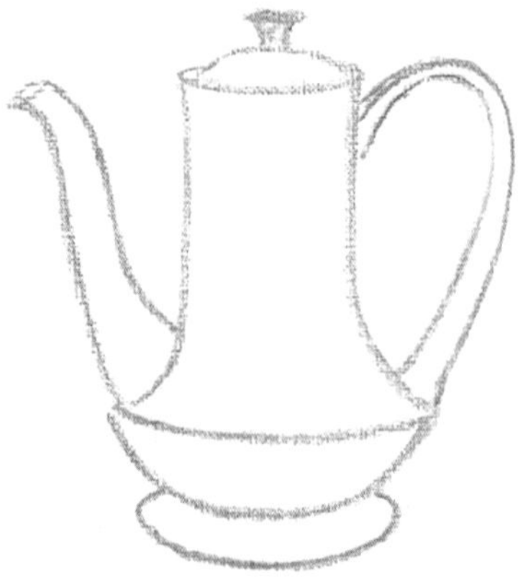

1. Charcoal sketch

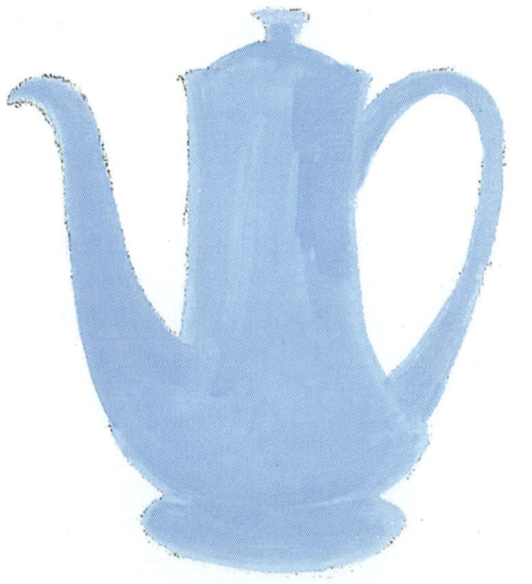

2. Light tone

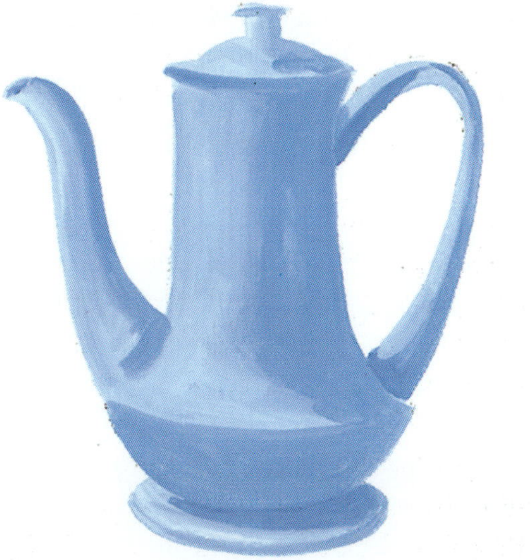

3.Medium tone

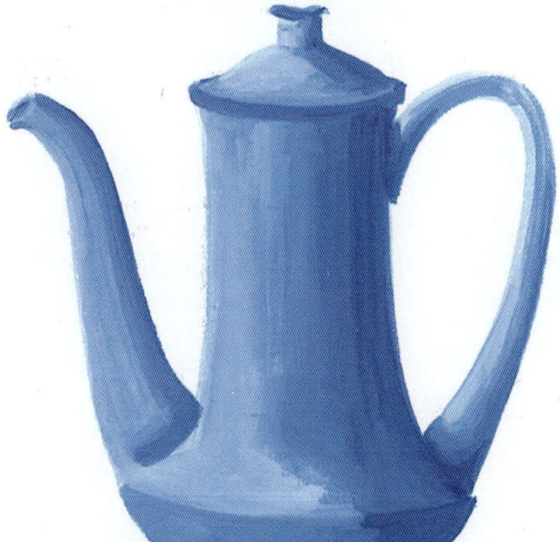

4. Dark tone

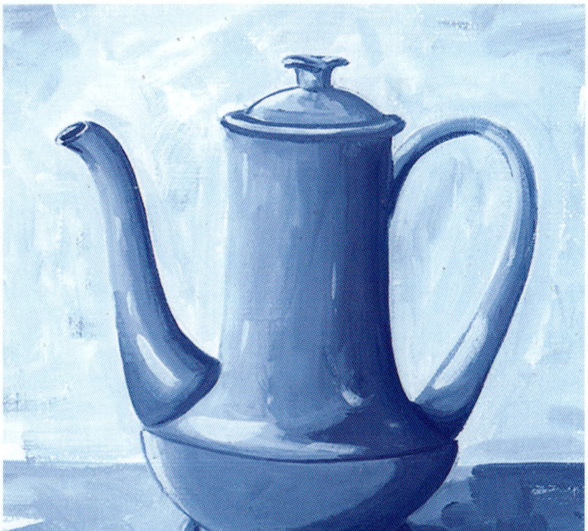

5. A finished jug

LANDSCAPE

Here is an easy, straightforward landscape for you to try using a range of colors. Do not forget to have a color chart by your side.

1. Draw the subject using either the charcoal or paintbrush drawing technique.

2. Paint each area of this painting using the *alla prima* technique—where the paint is used thickly and each area is completed while the paint is still wet. With a large bristle brush, paint in the blue of the sky using french ultramarine and white. Add clouds with a speck of yellow ochre to the white paint. Paint the pale gray cloud shadows using a little blue and brown mixed with white on your palette.

3. Continue with the above technique for the other areas of the landscape. Mix pale mauve and pale blue for the distant hills. Note how the green hills and fields are paler in the distance, becoming stronger in color and tone.

Mix pale mauve and pale blue for the distant hills. The green hills and fields are paler in the distance, becoming stronger in color and tone as they come nearer to the foreground. I have used greens made from french ultramarine, cadmium yellow and white. I don't like mixing black into a color to make the darker tones; instead I add a little near-black made from a mixture of burnt umber and french ultramarine. This is the method you should use for making the dark greens in this picture. Now add hedges and trees. Make the road using burnt umber and white—the darker tones for the road made with the brown/blue, black substitute. Use a flat or filbert brush for the walls and roof of the building.

4. Put in the details of the windows, door, chimneys, near hedges and fence, and add detail to the edges of the roadway using your round No. 3 detail brush.

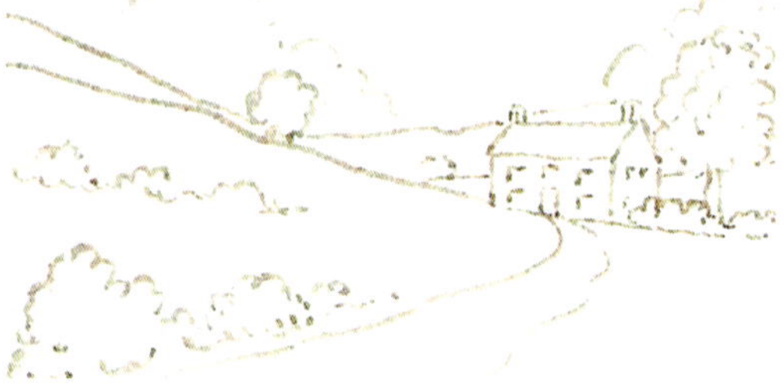

1. Sketching

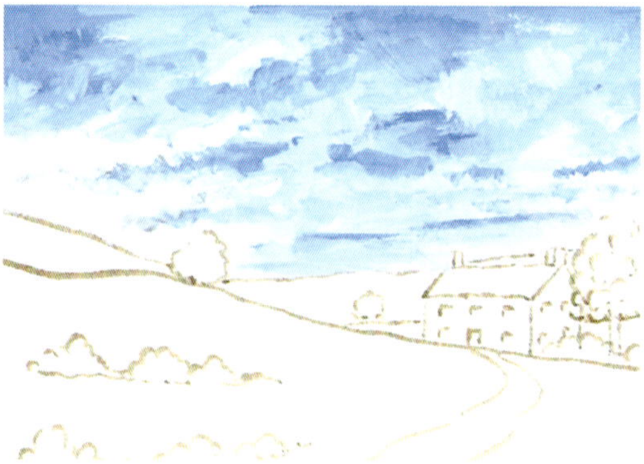

2. Painting alla prima

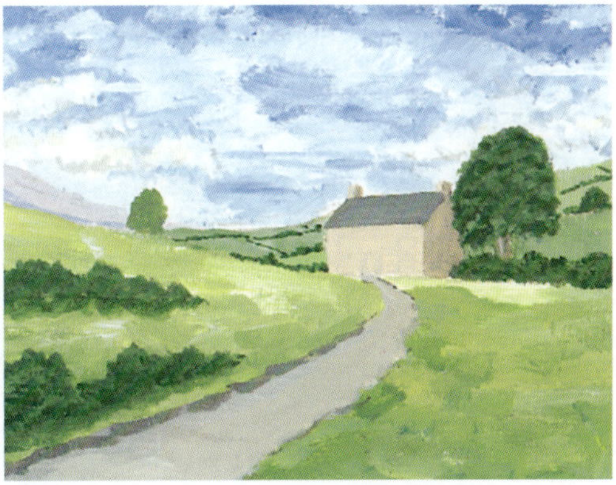

3. Painting for depth

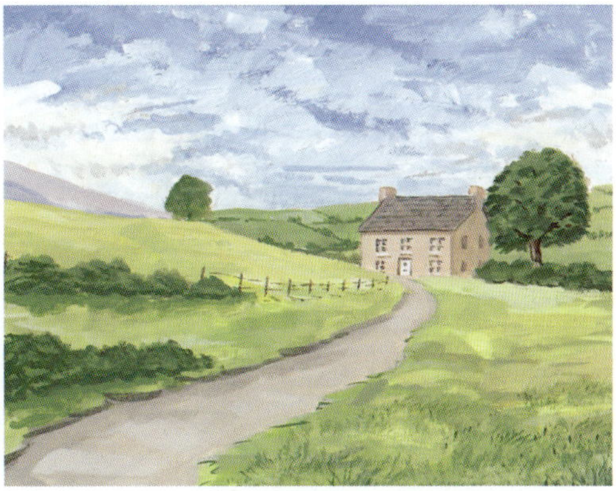

4. Painting for detail

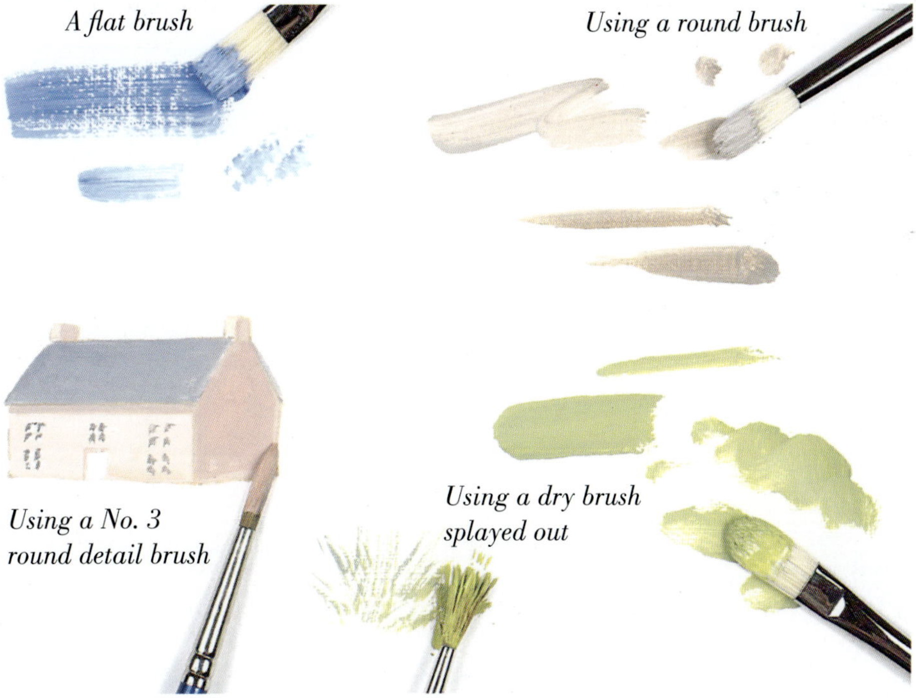

Brush marks and effects

SKIES

The next group of demonstrations is designed to help you explore painting skies using a range of different colors and atmospheric effects. They can be painted on either a square or rectangular painting board or support.

A Blue Summer Sky

1. Sketch the subject. Mix a little cerulean blue with white oil paint. Paint the sky using a stronger blue at the top, gradually lightening it as the sky comes down to the horizon. This is achieved by increasing the amount of white added to the blue mixture.

2. Use the thin side edge of the filbert brush and white paint to add the fleeting white clouds.

3. Add the green landscape using the same method used in the previous demonstration.

Stormy Sky

1. Paint a light mixture of cerulean blue and white into the top right-hand corner.. Mix prussian blue and a little white for the storm clouds.

2. Add a little burnt umber to the prussian blue and white mixture you have used. Paint in the very dark, deep base area of the storm clouds.

3. Paint the back row of industrial buildings in a deep mauve silhouette. Add the silhouette to the foreground building in a darker mauve by adding a little burnt umber and french ultramarine to the mauve. Finally, add the wisp of white smoke from the factory chimney.

Sunset

1. Paint white for the sun. Use lemon yellow mixed with white for the area immediately around the sun.

2. From the edges of the yellow, paint and blend in orange, made by mixing together red and yellow paint. Add alizarin crimson to the orange for the deeper red of the sky. Paint the clouds in mauve.

3. Paint in the silhouetted landscape using a mixture of mauve, french ultramarine and burnt umber.

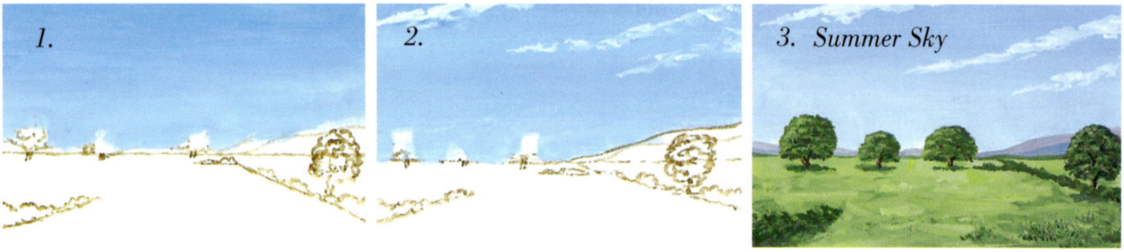

1.

2.

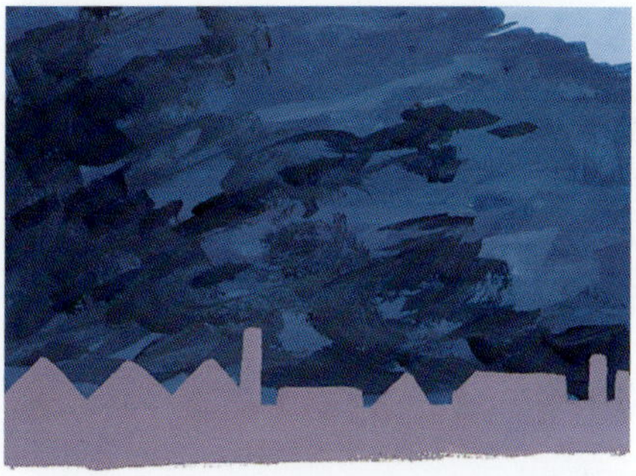

3.

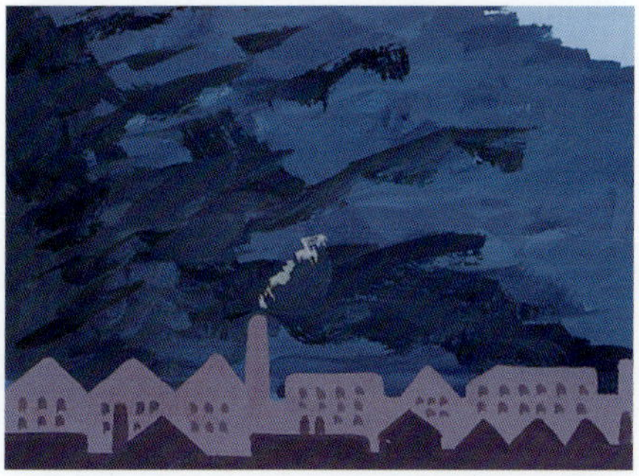

1.

2.

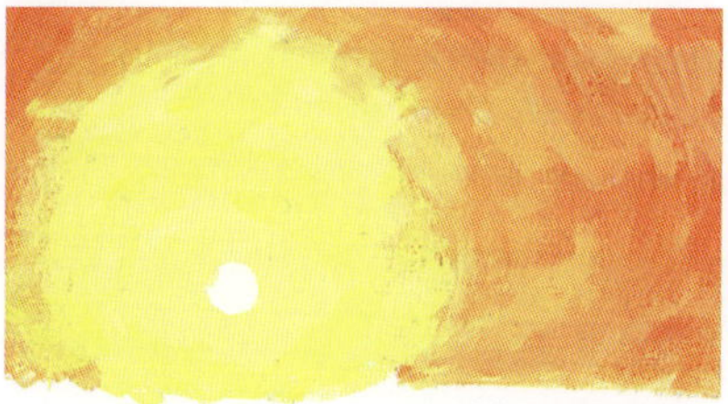

3.

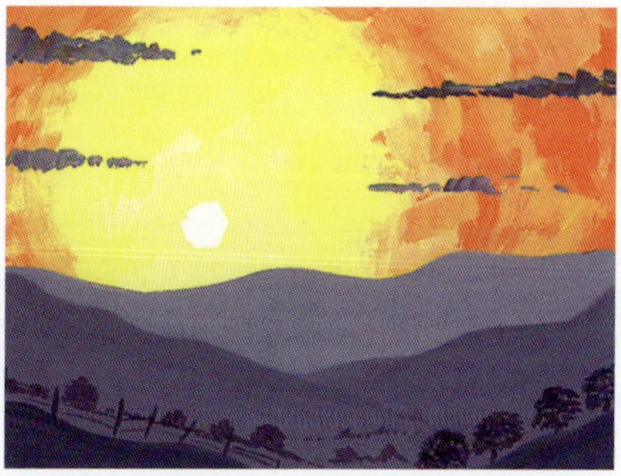

Stages for painting a stormy sky or a sunset

LANDSCAPE II

Allow each stage to become touch dry, which will take two to three days. To start, paint a first coat of each main color throughout the picture. Let the first coat become touch-dry. Then paint over the first coat of color with a second layer of each color. With the second layer, the paint takes on a more robust look, and the more finished modeling of the picture takes place. Let the second coat become touch-dry, and then add details and embellishments. One advantage of this technique is that if you make a mistake in the second layer, or in adding the final details, the error wipes away with a clean cloth dampened with a little turpentine. The area of the painting under the mistake will remain unspoiled, with the correction painted on top. When using this technique I often painting two pictures, working on the second picture on the days the first painting dries.

1. Draw the subject with charcoal, or a paintbrush technique.

2. Paint the first undercoat of color for each area—the sky, mountains, fields, lake and main trees. Let it become touch-dry.

3. Paint a second coat of each color for these areas, but adding the light and shade and thus modelling the picture. The paint layer will look more robust.

4. Add the detail to the trees, hedges and rocks in the lake and fence with the smaller brushes, including the No. 3 softer, round brush.

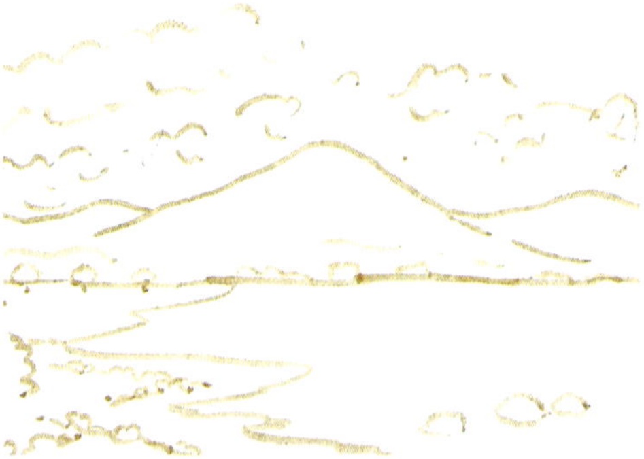

1. Sketch

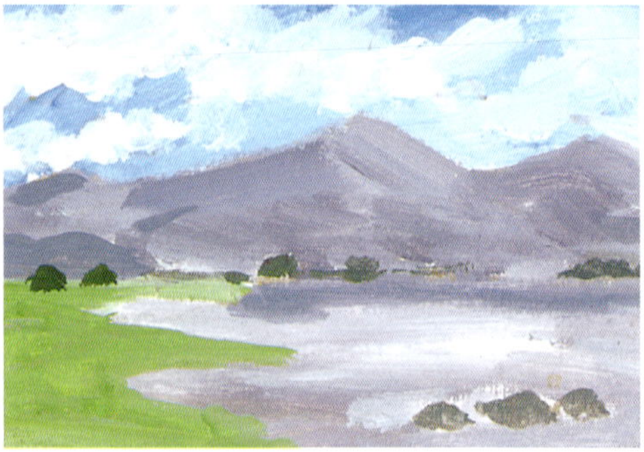

2. Paint a coat

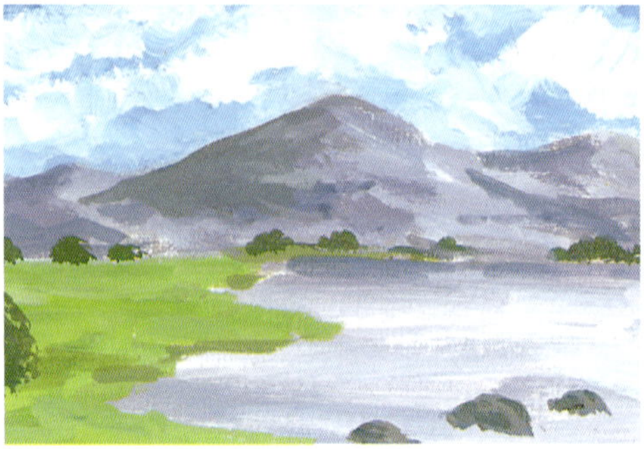

3. Add another count

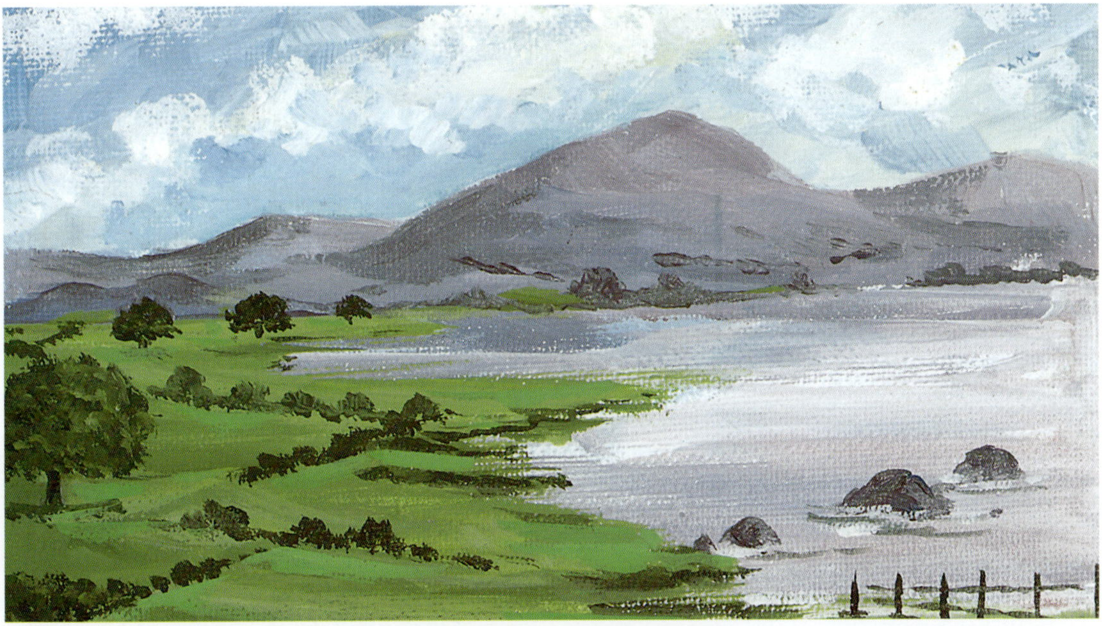

4. Continue to add detail

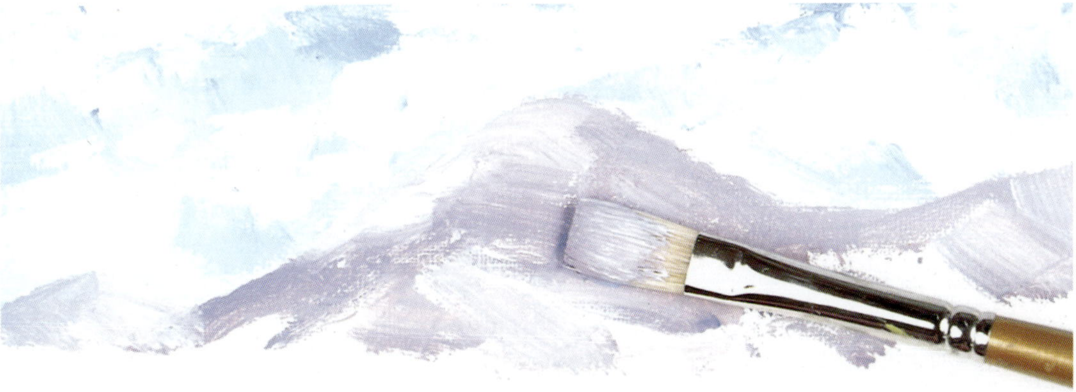

A close-up of brush strokes

LANDSCAPE III

Some of the most spectacular subjects occur in nature. A snow-covered winter landscape is just such an example, providing the subject for this demonstration.

1. Sketch the subject.

2. Mix together french ultramarine, burnt umber and white. Use a large flat brush to paint the blue area of the sky. This covers the upper area of the main tree and the edges of the distant trees. Mix a gray-brown from the above color for the background winter trees. The color of the bridge stonework derives from yellow ochre, white and dull green, by mixing blue with some yellow ochre and white. Increase the amount of blue and brown in the mixture for the darker colored underside of the bridge. Burnt sienna, yellow ochre, the dark green mixture and a little white make the various colors for the dead grass and blacken around the sides and front of the riverbank just in front of the bridge. A pale blue mixed with white creates the color for the river under the bridge and the lighter foreground areas. A darker, almost black-brown comprise the darker areas of the river. The main tree trunk is a mixture of burnt umber with yellow ochre and white for the lighter left-hand side, with an increase of blue and brown in the mixture for the darker right-hand side and branches. The larger areas of snow are a mixture of white paint with a touch of yellow ochre. The blue-mauve shadows on the snow are a mixture of white with a little alizarin crimson and french ultramarine. Let this become touch-dry. Shadows on the snow are a mixture of white with a little alizarin crimson and french ultramarine. Let this become touch-dry.

3. Using a darker tone of the colors used for the bridge in stage 1, add a suggestion of the stonework to the bridge. Use a medium dark gray-brown mixture on the tip of a fan brush, or a dry flat brush, to create a suggestion of more detail to the distant trees. See detail panel.

4. Mix together burnt umber, french ultramarine and a little white with turpentine to an inky consistency. Paint in the boughs and fine branches of the main tree using a No. 3 round detail brush. Add the rustic fence.

5. Add the bluish-white snow to the top of the bridge and fence. Pick out the white and darker toned brown grasses peeking through the snow on the banks of the river with a No. 3 detail brush.

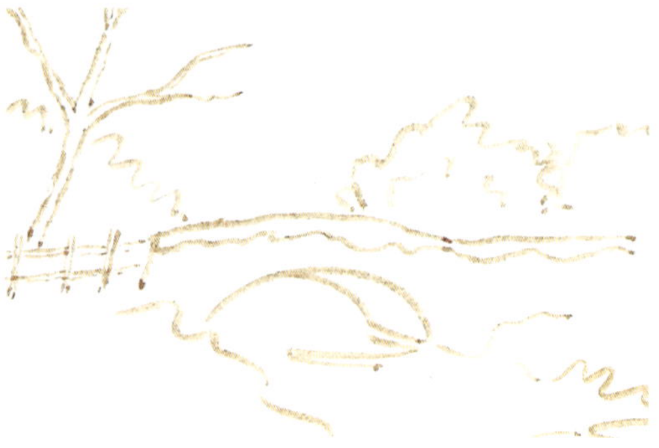

1. Sketching

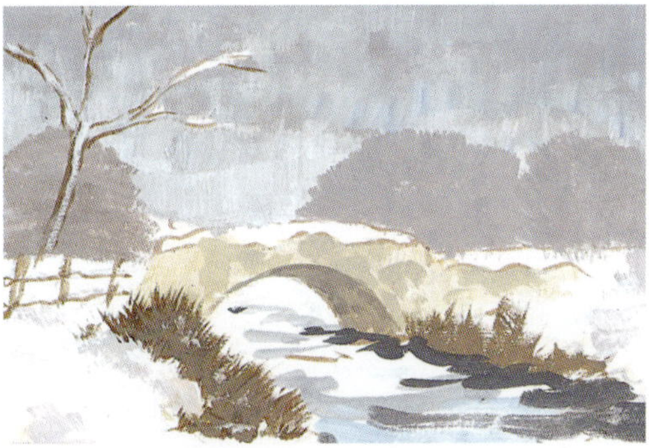

1. Painting touch dry

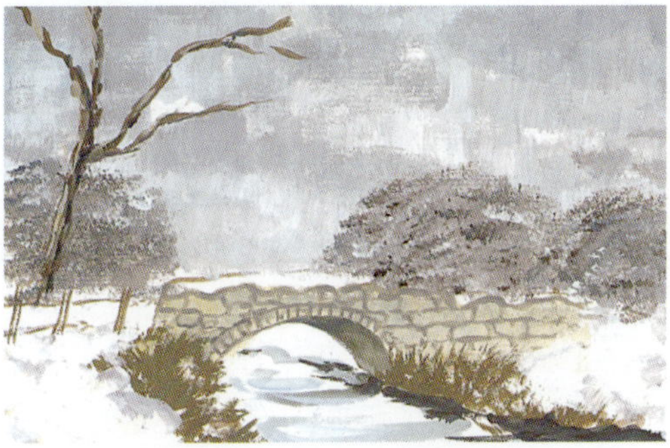

2. Adding detail

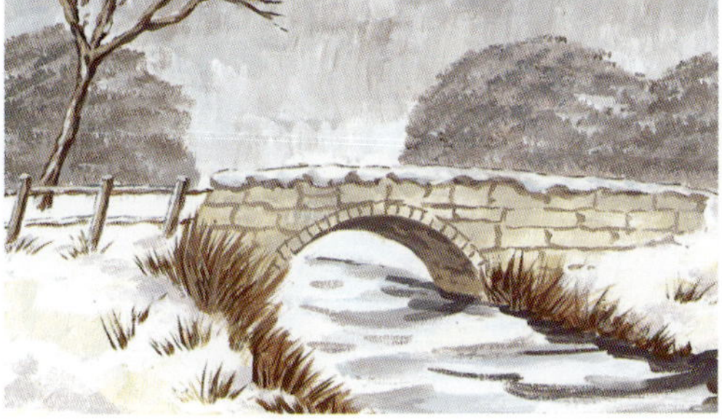

3. More detail to finish

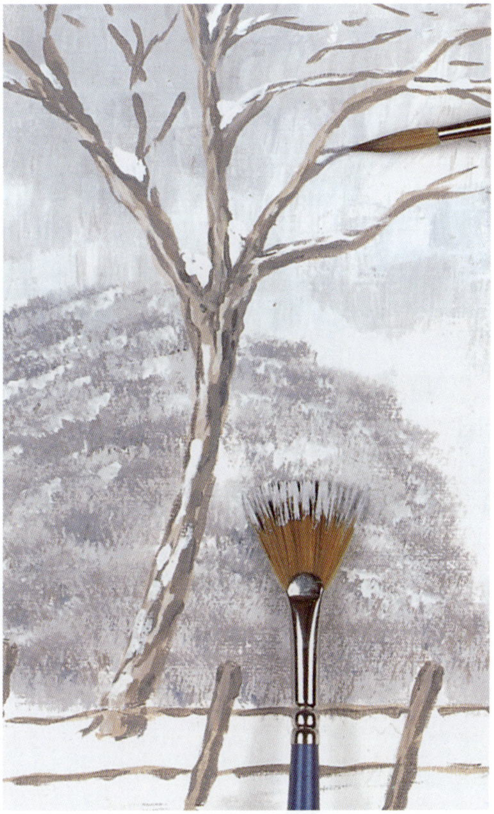

Detail of brushwork

TEDDY BEAR

There are many interesting and exciting subjects all around us. I found this colorful selection in our child's bedroom. I placed the teddy bear against a pillow and assembled the ball, drum and building bricks to make a triangular composition on the bed.

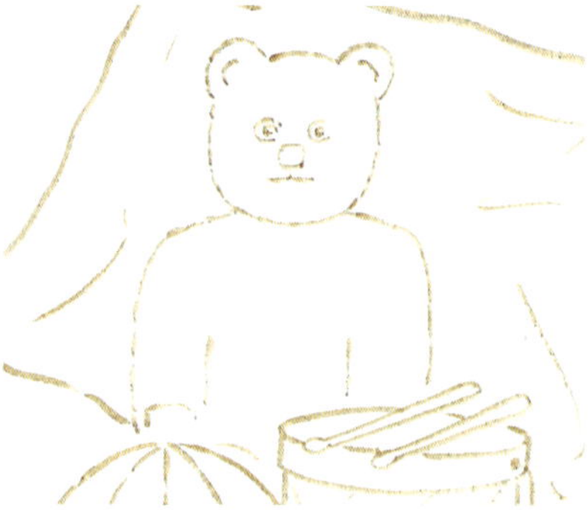

1. Sketching

1. Sketch the subject.

2. Build the painting up to the almost finished stage using the methods learned in the previous demonstrations.

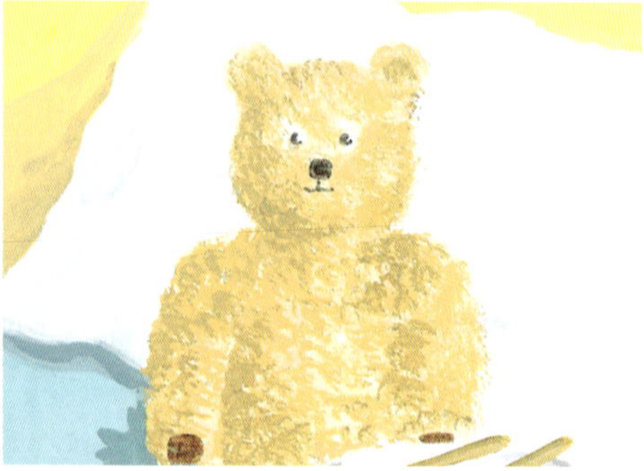

2 Building with paint

3. The addition of the essential detail is particularly important in the final stage of this painting, and the picture should be touch-dry before adding detail. Pay careful attention to the teddy bear's eyes and nose, ensuring the dark pupils are almost black, and pick out the white highlights of the eyes. Use a fan brush, or a very dry hog bristle brush, to increase the texture of the teddy bear's fur. Use a darker tone of yellow ochre and burnt umber mixed into the beige paint on the tip of the brush. Touch and flick the brush to catch the surface of the dry, painted fur using the dry brush technique.

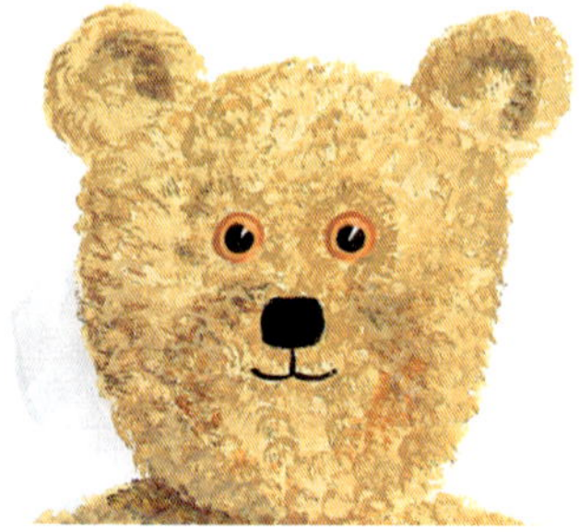

3. Getting the white in the eyes

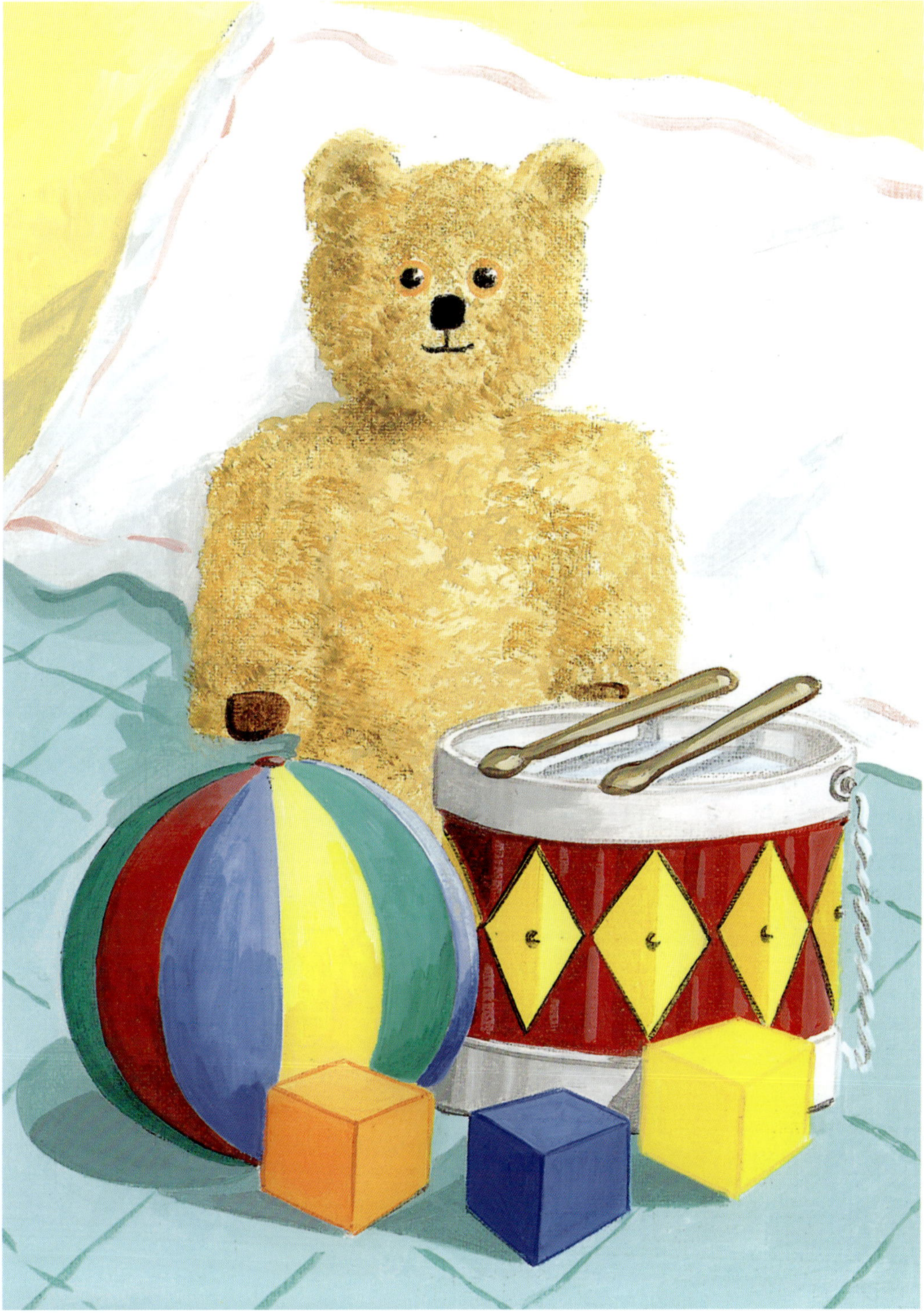

FLOWER

To achieve success in flower painting, start simply by learning to paint individual flowers, ideally from life rather than from photographs. Keep a sketchbook and, as the seasons come round, make sketches of flowers as they come into bloom. Also, make oil painted sketches of the flowers and keep notes about the colorings. By doing this you will come to learn about the makeup, line, form and characteristics of many flowers. This will lead to a confident approach when you decide to paint larger groups and arrangements of flowers. The technique shown here is an ideal method for the painting of flowers:

1. Draw the daffodil and tulip and start to block in the main colors. Use lemon yellow with white for the daffodil head, alizarin crimson and white to make a pink for the tulip head. Mix french ultramarine and cadmium yellow with white for the stems and leaves.

2. Mix a little green with the yellow and paint in the shadows on the petals and trumpet of the daffodil. Add a little blue to the pink mixture and paint in the shadows on the tulip head. Likewise, paint in a darker green mixture for the shadows on the stem and leaves. At this point, let the study become touch-dry.

3. Use your No. 3 detail brush and a darker tone of each color previously used to pick out the detail of the daffodil head, the frilly end of the trumpet, the essential edges of the daffodil petals and the darker edges of the tulip petals. Also, pick out any key lines on the leaves. Show the stamens of the daffodil and, finally, clearly identify and paint in any highlights.

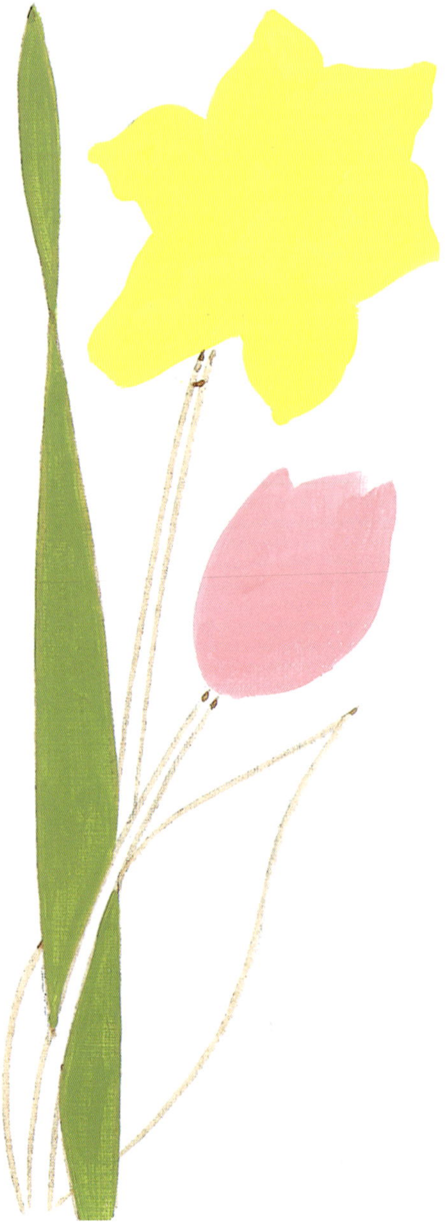

1. Draw and paint to block in later

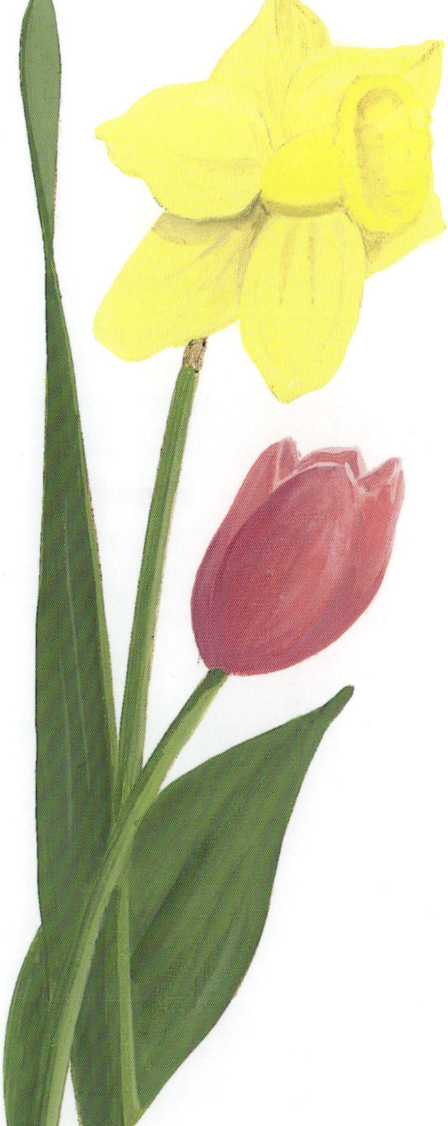

2. Paint in the shadows

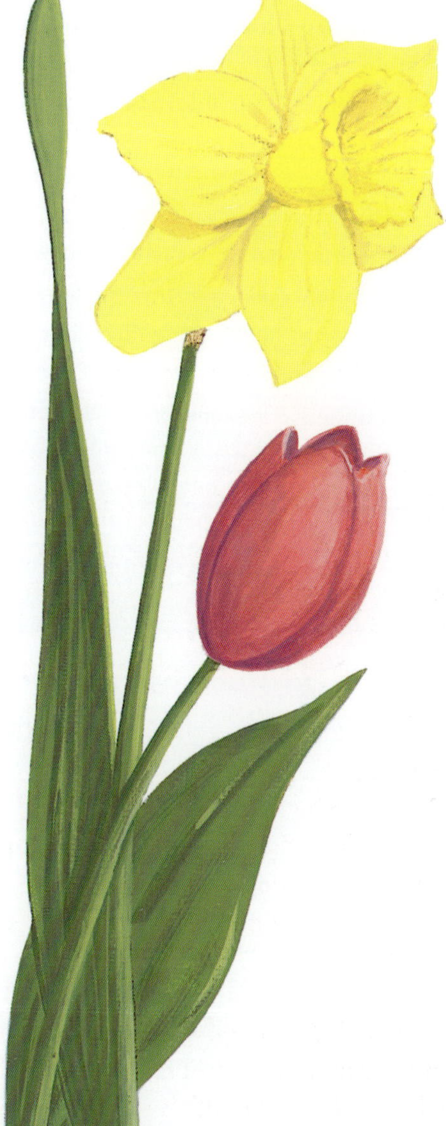

3. Add detail with color

THE ARCHER

While on a painting expedition to the Isle of Man, I visited Castle Rushen. Among the superb tableaux, I found this full-sized model of an archer on guard in the guardhouse. I used this subject in my television series, and produced this demonstration for you to try.

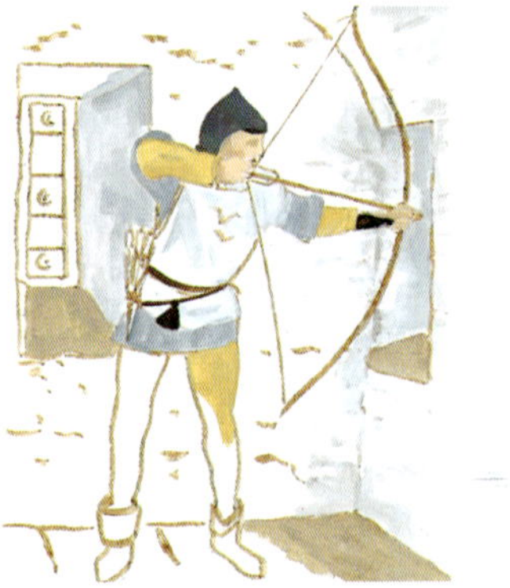

1. Sketch the archer

1. Sketch out the archer. Start to block in the gray helmet, yellow ochre sleeves and brown and beige tights. Also, add the gray chain mail vest showing just below the white sleeveless top. Make the flesh color for the face and hands by mixing a little alizarin crimson, yellow ochre and white. Mix white with a trace of blue and paint in the background walls. Paint in the gray floorboards and window areas. Leave the painting to become touch-dry.

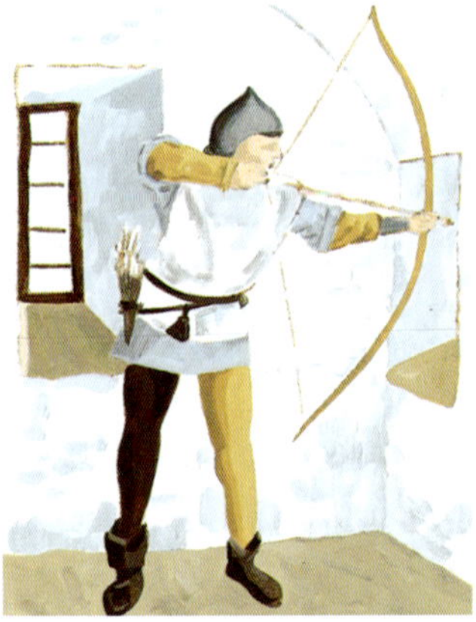

2. First layer of paint

2. Paint over each area with their main colors, but concentrating on painting in the light, medium and dark tones for each item and area. Leave the painting to become touch-dry.

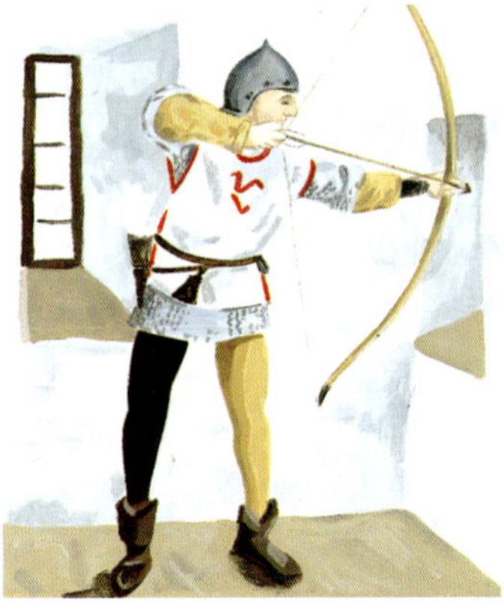

3. Adding detail

3. Use your fine brush to pick out the details on the face, the decoration and designs of the helmet, white vest, belt, moneybag, quiver of arrows, longbow and arrow. Add the semicircular marks on the chain-mail garment.

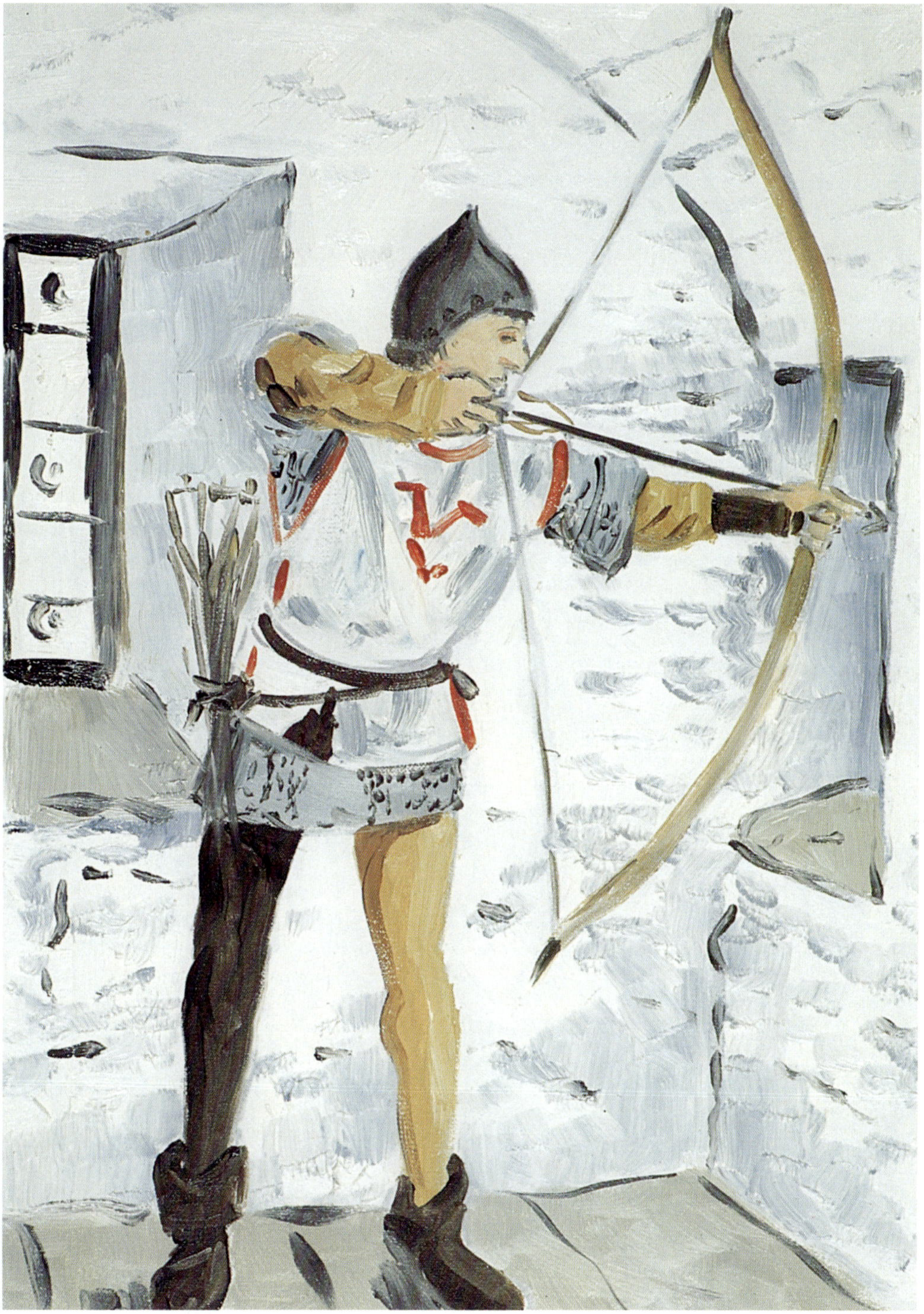

A FOAL

The painting of the foal "June" is a particular favorite of mine. A farmer asked if I would paint her, as she was the family pet on which his granddaughters were learning to ride. This was an interesting challenge. There were two main problems. First, animals do not stand still to be painted. The second challenge was to capture her young look, the size of a foal, rather than a full-grown mare. I decided to paint a view looking from slightly above the foal. I made some sketches and color notes at the farm, and walked around the foal shooting a roll of film with my camera from different angles. I then used the original sketches and photographs to sketch and paint June in my studio to the nearly finished stage. I took the painting back to the farm. I looked again at the foal, compared her to my painting, and added the final details and final changes to the painting at the farm. Try painting June in the stages shown here:

1. Sketch out the foal.

2. Use a mix of yellow ochre, burnt sienna and white for the body, head, mane and ears. Use white for the flash on the front of the head. Use a mixture of french ultramarine and burnt umber for the hooves. Paint the nostrils and mouth area in blackish-gray made from the previous dark mix, with a little white added.

3. Ensure that you show the light and dark areas on the underside of the body, front of the neck, head and legs. Paint in the eye with your detail brush. Paint the brown leather harness using a mixture of burnt umber, french ultramarine and a little white. This mixture will allow you to achieve the light, medium and dark tones of the leather. Paint the brass rings using a mixture of lemon yellow, yellow ochre and white.

4. Now add the background—keep it simple to ensure the emphasis is on the foal. Achieve a greater sense of depth to the field by placing the distant hedge and tree high up in the picture, and by using a light mixture of cerulean blue and white for the sky. Utilize the light green of the field in the distance and the stronger green and shadow cast by the foal in the foreground.

Make the greens for the field from a mixture of cadmium yellow, lemon yellow and french ultramarine with white. Create the darker greens by adding a little more blue and brown to the green paint mixture.

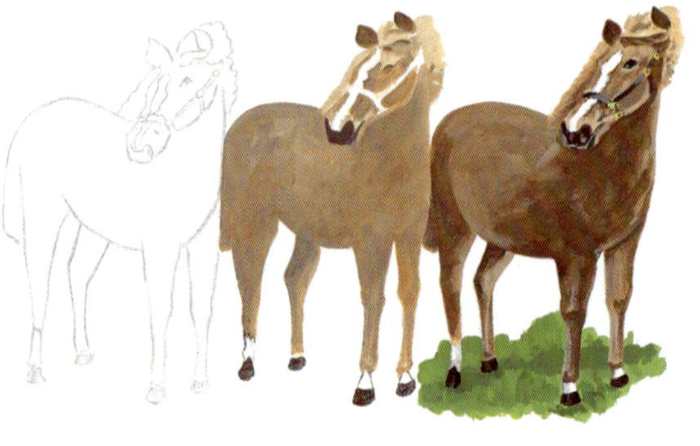

Stages of painting, overlapped

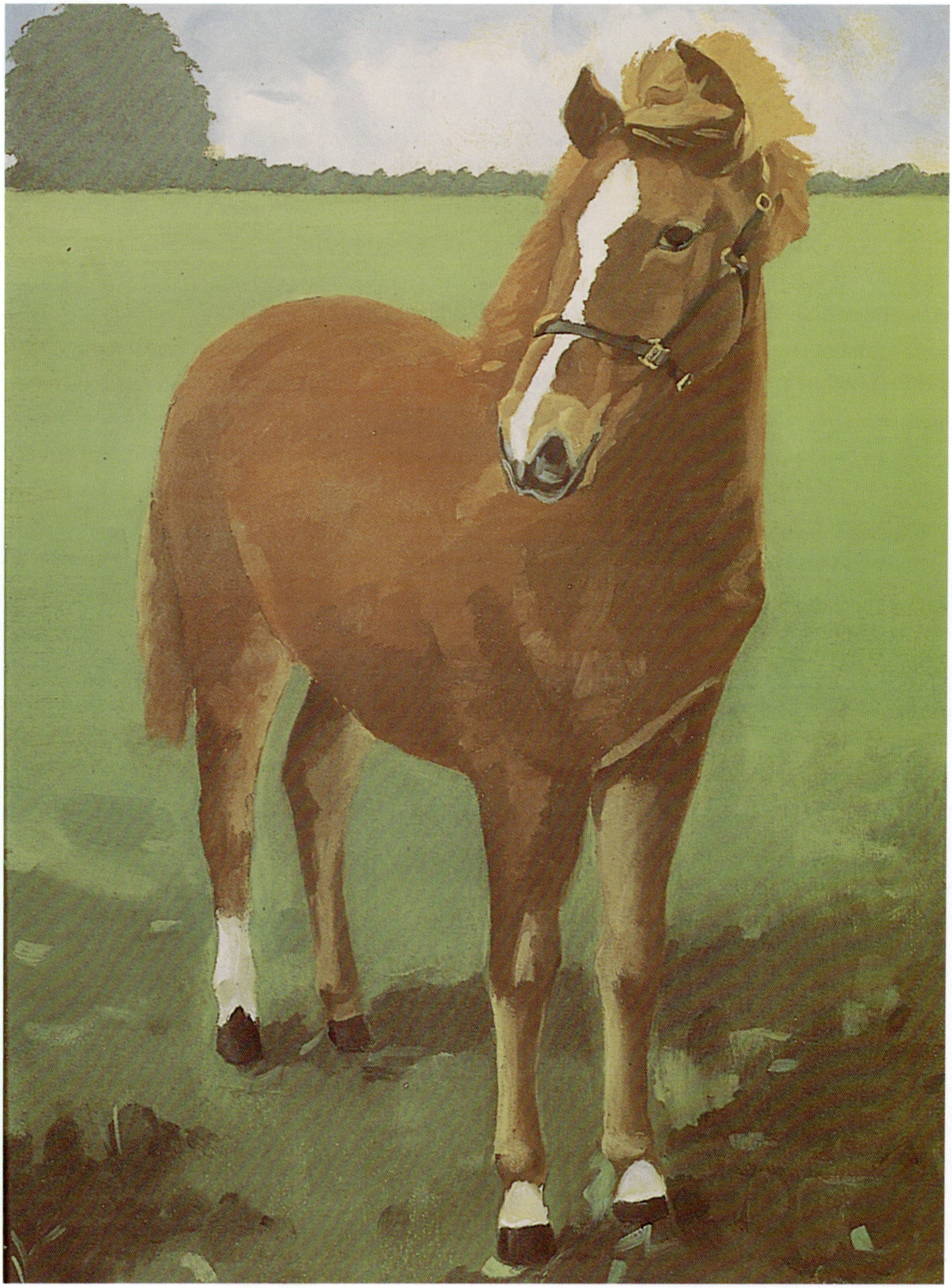

VENICE

Venice has had a profound influence on me, as it has on artists, writers, poets and musicians over the centuries. Venice is liquid light. The sunlight and the varying skies, and the light reflected by water, create stunning effects during all four seasons of the year. The narrow streets, the canals with their bridges, the gondolas, the open squares, palaces, markets and the Venetian citizens, make for a wealth of material.

The view from St. Mark's Square to the island of San Giorgio Maggiore is one of the best-known in Europe. A mass of gondolas waiting for the day's tourists to arrive, and to glide them along the canals of Venice, cluttered the waterfront when I arrived. I decided to reduce the number of gondolas to see more of the main view, and to use the perspective lines of the paving stones to bring sight onto the main focal point of the picture, San Maggiore, across the water. I also decided to use the gondola mooring posts to intersect the buildings, which in turn helped to link the foreground and the distance; this ensured that the picture did not cut into two equal horizontal halves.

1. Draw the subject firmly in charcoal on a canvas or canvas board. Use a dry cloth and vigorously dust off the loose charcoal. This should leave a clear drawing for you to paint your picture.

2. For the sky, use cerulean blue and white. For the brick color of the buildings, use burnt sienna and white. Make white and pale grays of the stone by mixing white, french ultramarine and burnt umber.

The water is a mixture of white, yellow ochre and a little viridian green. For the gondola hulls use a black and gray made from french ultramarine, burnt umber and, where needed, a little white. Make the gondola seat covers from white with a little lemon yellow and a touch of viridian green. Paint the mooring posts using burnt umber with a little white, the paving stones with yellow ochre and white with a little burnt umber. Use the same colors throughout the other stages of this painting. Use a No. 10 flat brush for the sky, water and paving stones, a No. 6 flat brush for the buildings and a No. 6 round brush for the gondolas and mooring posts.

3. When Stage 2 is touch-dry, paint over it with the main coat of paint for each area and item. Stage 2 is the under painting, Stage 3 is the main painting. Remix each color and apply the second coat, also painting in the fleeting clouds and the main water effects as shown in the detail panel. Let this stage become touch-dry. Add details carefully in the final stage.

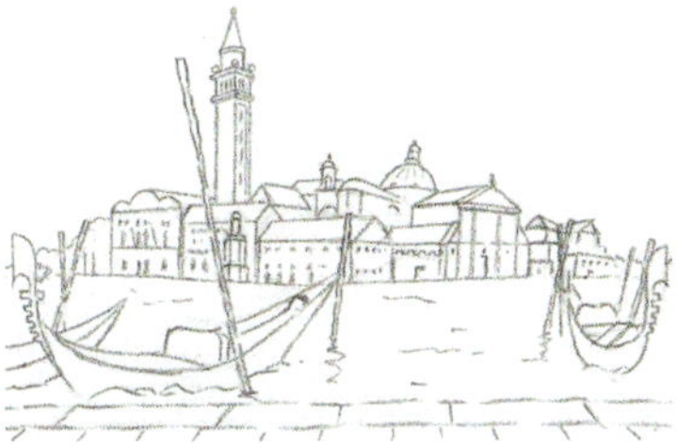

1. Sketch

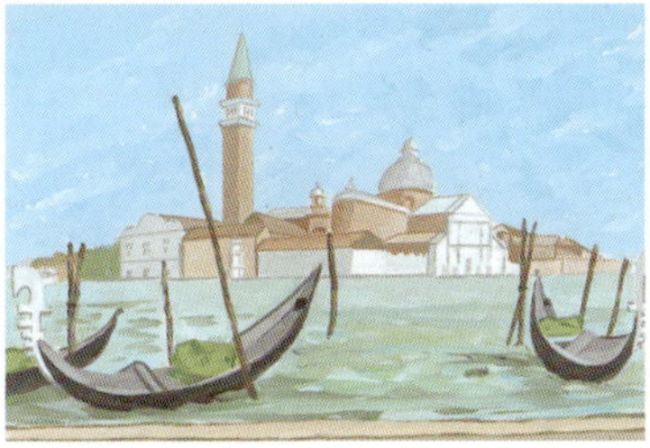

2. A layer of color

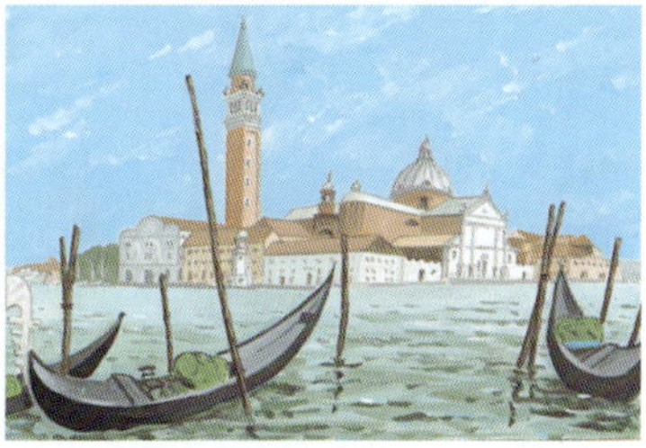

3. Build with paint

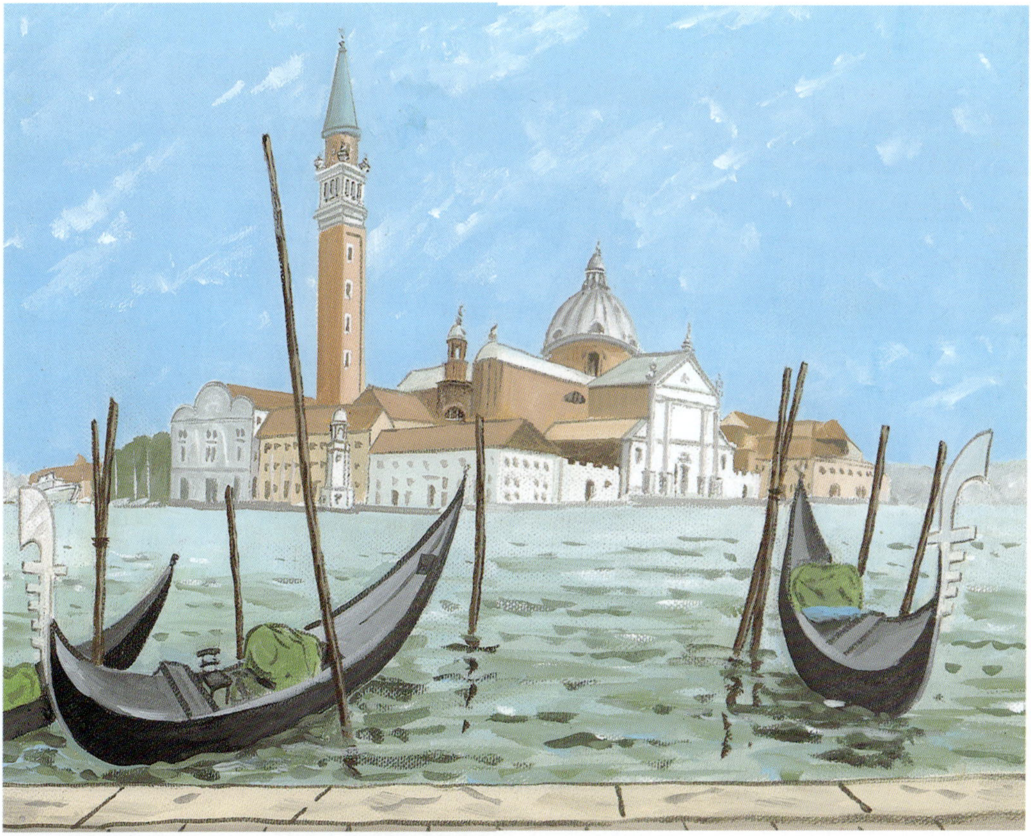

4. A finsihed view of Venice

PORTRAITURE

Many people who take up painting quite soon find they can produce some quality work and have an urge to try a portrait. Some people will have a natural flair for portraits and others will find it more of a challenge. My advice is to avoid painting members of the family and children until you have gained expertise in painting character faces. People over the age of twenty-five, particularly older people, often have lines of character and distinctive features and provide the best subjects. After gaining experience on these types of faces, family faces can be tried. The difficulty in painting children, with their very smooth complexions, is trying to convey accurately the age of the young person. This is challenging but achievable with practice. In the portrait demonstration, I used as my model a rugged-looking local builder. I always make a number of quick pencil sketches to decide on the best view: full face, profile, or, as here, a three-quarter view.

1. Sketch the face using the charcoal drawing method.

2. Paint the face and neck using a medium flesh tone made from a little yellow ochre, alizarin crimson and white. The hair is a mixture of burnt umber, a little yellow ochre and white. Block in the shirt using cerulean blue and white. The lumber jacket uses yellow ochre, burnt umber and white.

3. Mix a little alizarin crimson with the flesh color used in Stage 2 for the cheeks. Add a little french ultramarine and alizarin crimson to the flesh color for the jaw and shadow on the neck. Sometimes the addition of a very small amount of viridian green to the flesh mixture can make a good flesh shadow color. Pick out the lighter and darker tones of the hair. Allow the painting to become touch-dry.

4. Using your No. 3 round detail brush, add the eyes with a pale blue and a bluish-black mixture for the pupils. Use burnt umber with a little blue added to paint in the eyebrows, nostril and moustache. Add a darker flesh tone for the shadow under the lip. Add more detail to the shirt and jacket. Do not however let the detail in the clothes dominate the face.

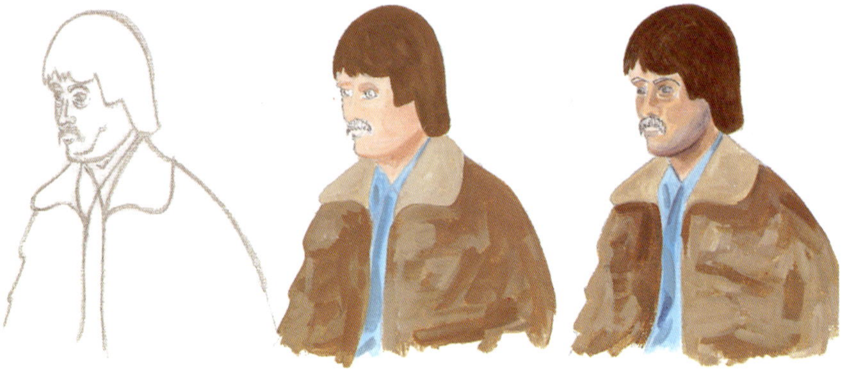

Stages for creating a portrait

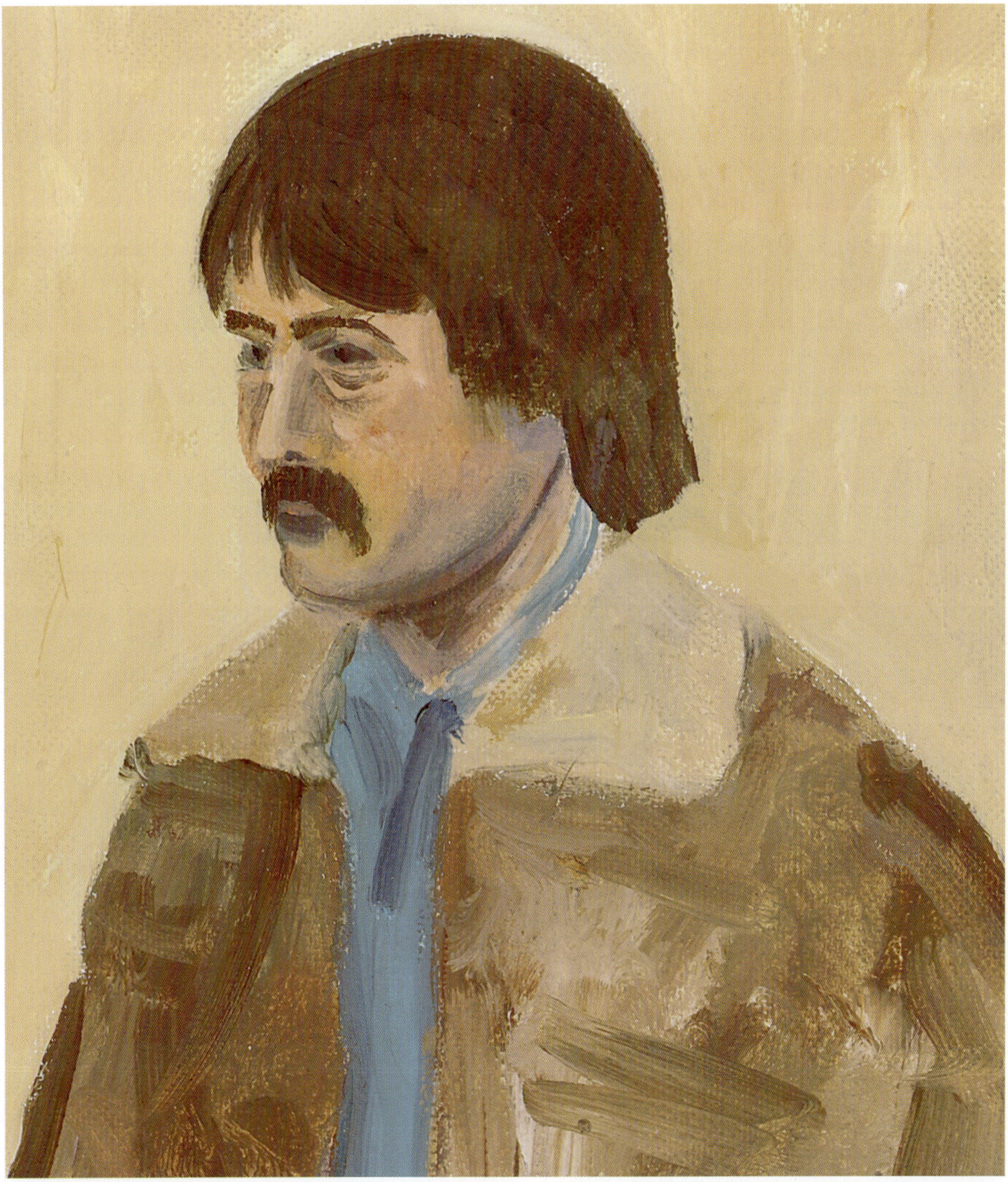

THE CAMERA

Some artists say never copy from photographs; others say it is fine to do so. Often, people ask what is right. A camera can be an invaluable tool for an artist. When I go out sketching, I usually take my camera with me. A combination of sketches, with the back-up reference of photographs, provides everything needed to produce one or more paintings in the studio. Sometimes, if outdoors, or on holiday with family and friends, I see a subject I would love to paint, but there is not even time to make a sketch. The camera provides a quick snapshot of the subject for later use.

If you happen to be housebound, photographs can provide a regular source of material. Do not copy the photograph slavishly, however. Let your own style and interpretation of the subject come through in the painting.

You will often find a subject within a subject. Here I show a photograph of a Scottish harbor and I also show three boxes or sections that could result from this photograph, as pictures in their own right. This offers you the choice of painting the whole view, or any one of the three segments, in the way shown in my finished painting.

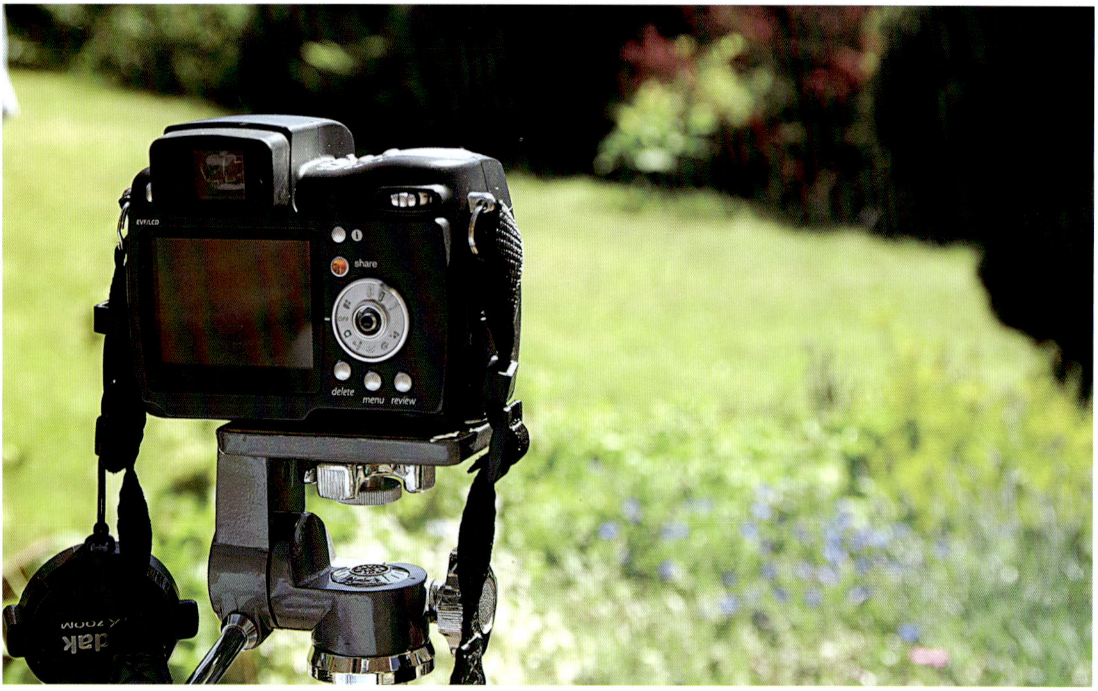

The camera: a part of the painter's craft

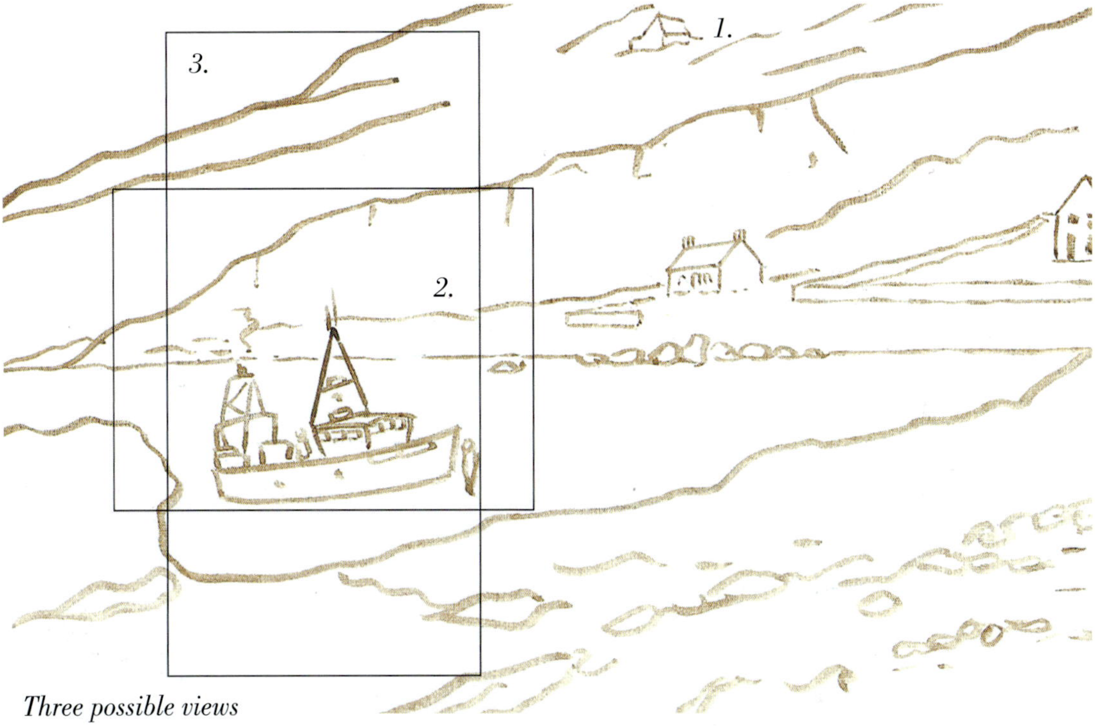

Three possible views

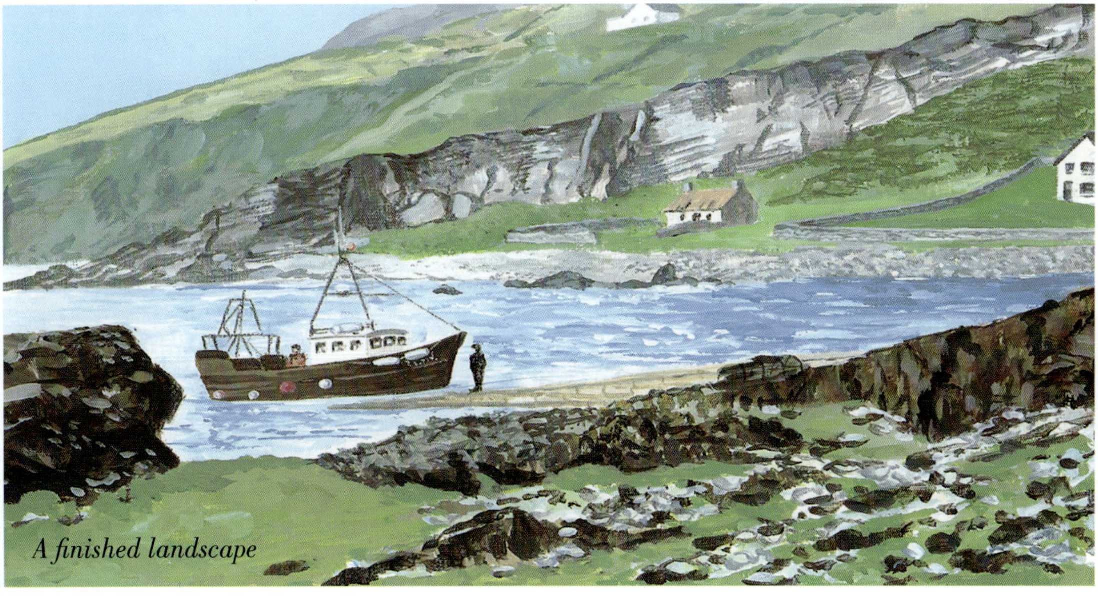

A finished landscape

PAINTING OUTDOORS

Many people think oil paints are not a suitable medium for outdoor use due to the wet, sticky nature of the painting. It can be practical, if you have a car, to transport the wet paintings and your equipment to the location and back. Some art stores sell canvas carrier devices for holding wet oil paintings. If you are on holiday, however, or do not have a car available, there are two practical methods I use for outdoor oil painting which could be of help to you.

Liquin

Liquin, an alkyd resin, can mix with your oil paints instead of turpentine or linseed oil for normal oil painting techniques. It accelerates the drying of the oil paint. I use it frequently. If I am on holiday and use liquin to mix with my oil paint when painting at the beginning of the holiday, the pictures are touch-dry at the end of the holiday and can, with care, transport home safely. Griffin alkyd paints are synthetic paints similar to oils but based in alkyd resin. They are normally touch-dry in about eighteen hours.

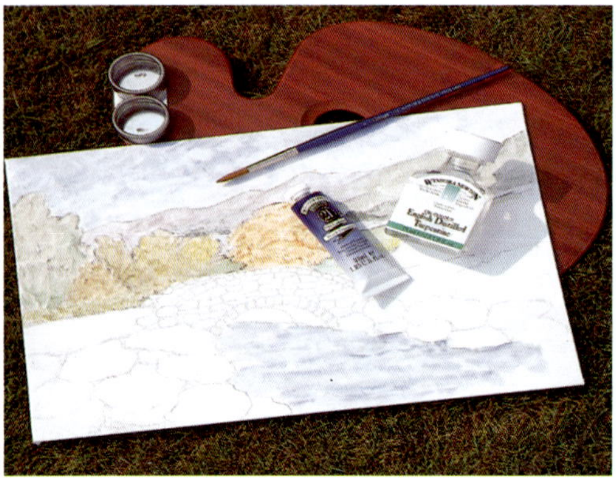

Materials for painting outdoors

The Tinted Canvas Panel

I took this photograph at the location where I painted my tinted canvas panel. I chose my final viewpoint more to the right so that it included more of the fast-running stream.

1. Take a canvas panel, your oil paints and materials out with you, making sure you have some clean turpentine. When you find an appealing subject, sketch it out in charcoal on the canvas panel.

2. Instead of using your oil paints thickly, as normal, do the opposite. Mix the paint thinly and tint the various colored areas of the subject, or view, with a thin tint of its own natural color.

3. With care, thinly apply the light, medium and dark tones of color for each part of the subject. The result will have an almost watercolor painting look to it. In thirty to sixty minutes the turpentine will have evaporated and the panel will be dry. You can then take the panel home. On cold, wet, winter days or dark evenings, sitting in the comfort of your home or studio, take the panel out and paint the fully finished oil painting on top of your original, tinted oil color panel.

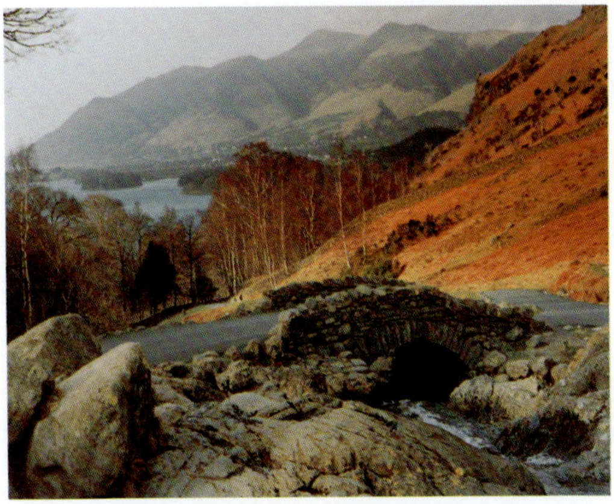

1. An original photograph

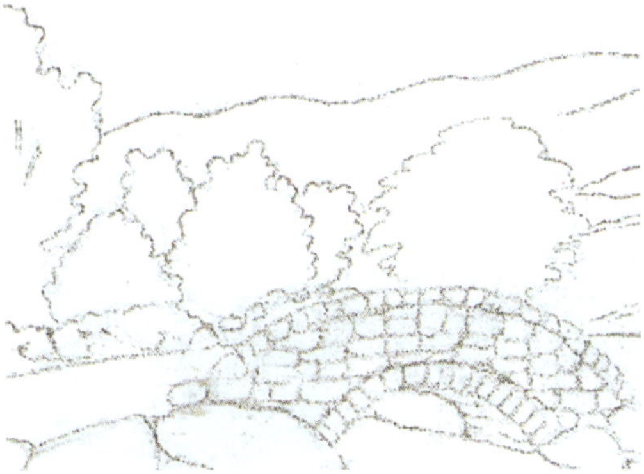

2. A sketch

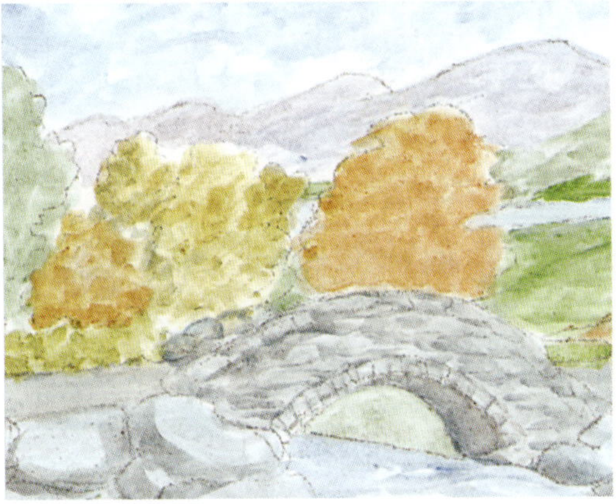

2. The first layer of paint

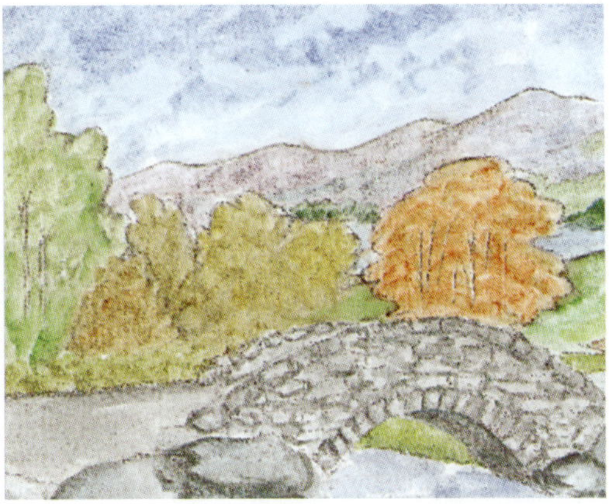

4. A finished painting

COMPOSITION

There are certain guidelines that, if followed, can help you build your work on sound compositional foundations. One of the most important things to avoid is having any line or object that cuts your picture into two equal halves. Set any such line or object to one side or other.

Focal Points and Key Lines

Decide what it is that you want the viewer to look at. Ensure their eyes will not wander, as if the viewer is lost. You are the artist, you are in control, be decisive.

A picture should have a focal point; that is, a main feature to which the eye may be drawn. I show three views. In the first example the focal point, the cottage, is in the middle distance. In the second example the focal point, the ship, is in the far distance. In the third the fisherman in the foreground is the focal point.

A picture should also have key lines of the composition leading the eyes of the viewer to the focal point. I have arrowed the key lines of the three compositions and I think from these illustrations you will see how the use of the focal point and key lines help bring a composition together.

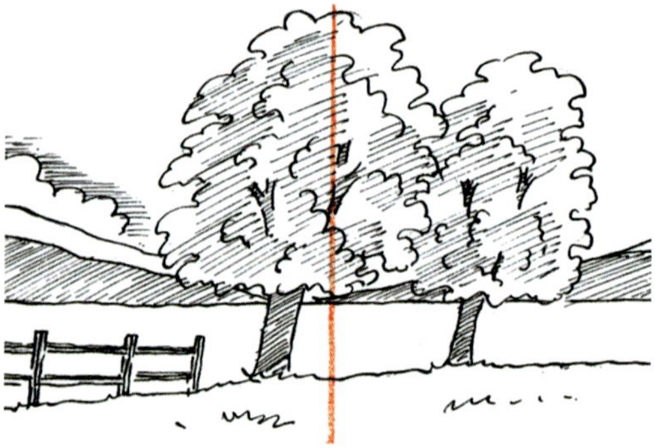

Halfway

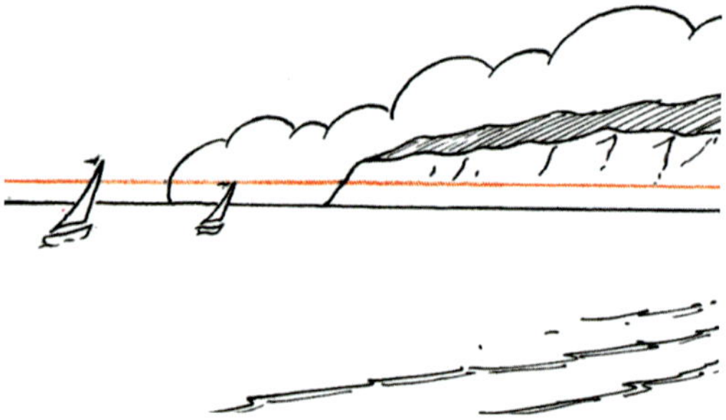

Halfway

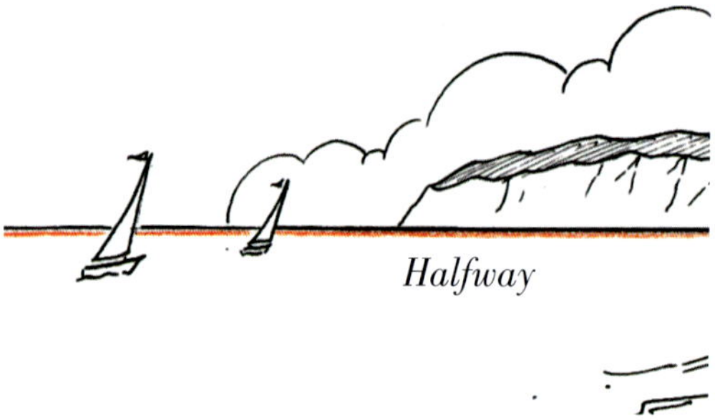

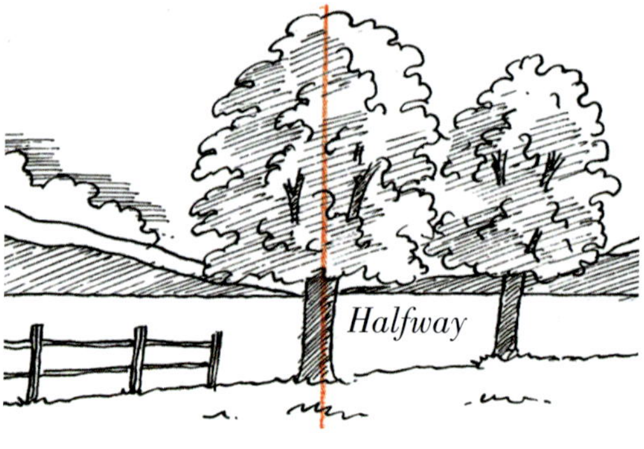

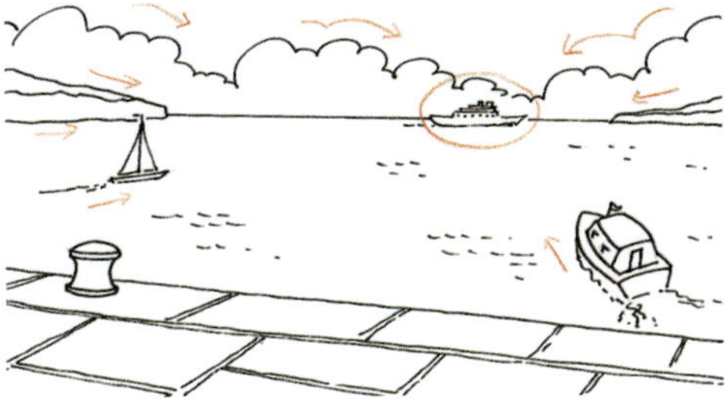

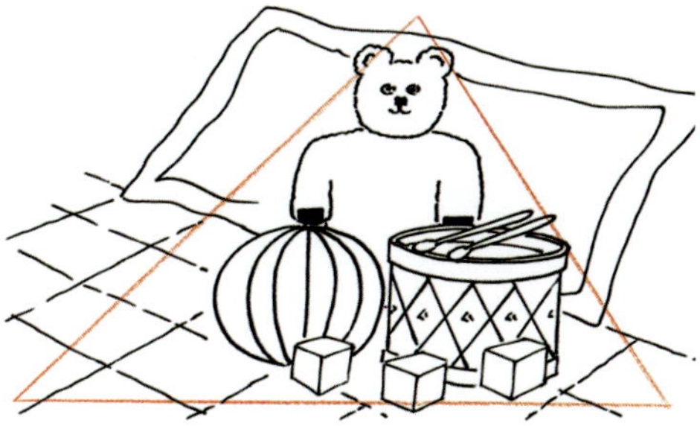

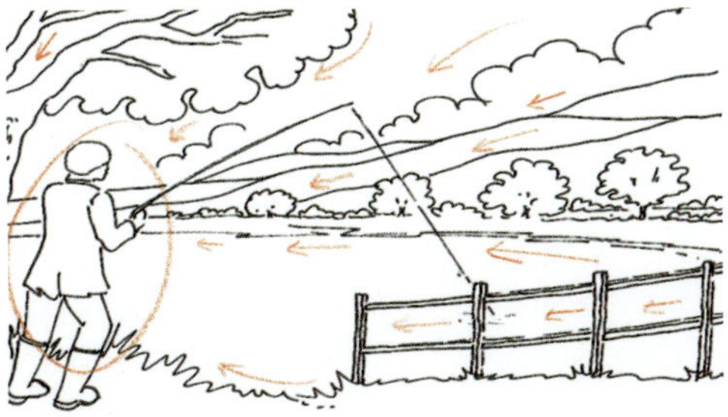

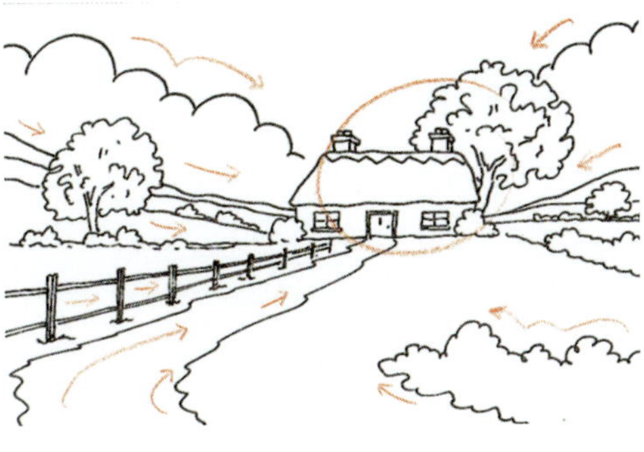

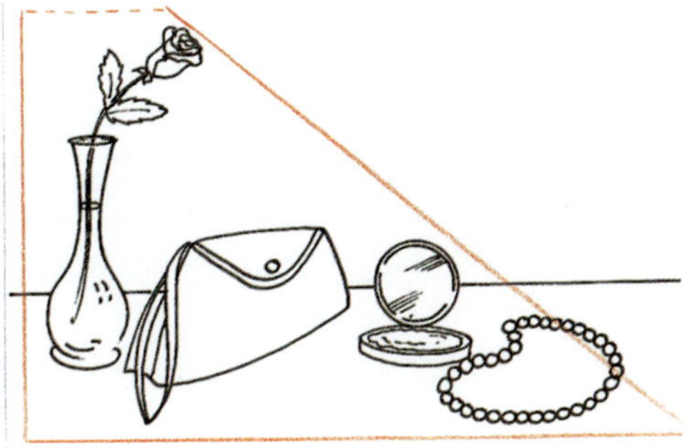

The Triangle

Often a triangle can offer an excellent shape on which to base a composition, especially a still life or floral study. I have a still life made up from a group of toys. I have placed the teddy bear to the right so the apex of the triangle is off-center. The rose in the vase forms the upright of the triangle, with the handbag and powder compact forming the base. The tree creates the triangle's upright side, with the landscape and church forming the bottom and third, sloping side, of the triangle. Try to ensure that still life and floral studies have height, width and depth to them. If you now go and look at paintings or prints of paintings by any of the great masters, or by any fine artist, you will almost certainly find that their most successful paintings employ many of the important compositional points that I have referred to here.

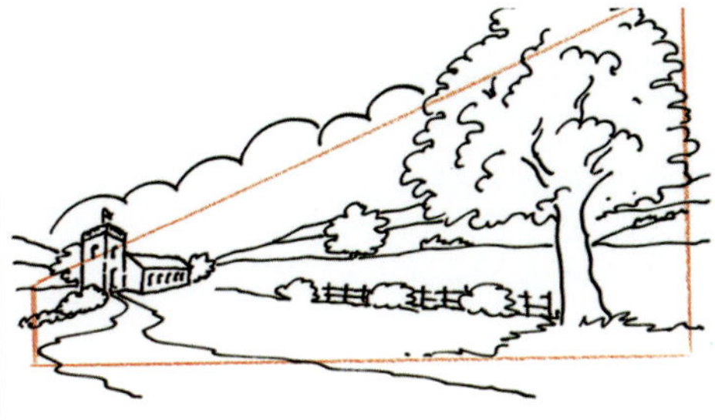

PERSPECTIVE

Perspective is the one area of drawing and painting with which most people experience some degree of difficulty. When most people hear perspective mentioned they go to a bookshop or a library, obtain a book on the subject, flip through it, see lines shooting about all over, and usually end up more confused than before. The secret is to keep the whole business of perspective as simple as possible, to remember a few basic rules and to bear in mind that perspective is not something one masters all in one, two or three lessons. Learning about perspective is an ongoing learning process. One goes along over a period of months or years, collecting together the pieces of information like pieces of a jigsaw, until they all fit together and the picture, the theory of perspective, becomes clear and easy to apply to one's work. This basic familiarity with line is very handy when learning to paint.

fig. 1

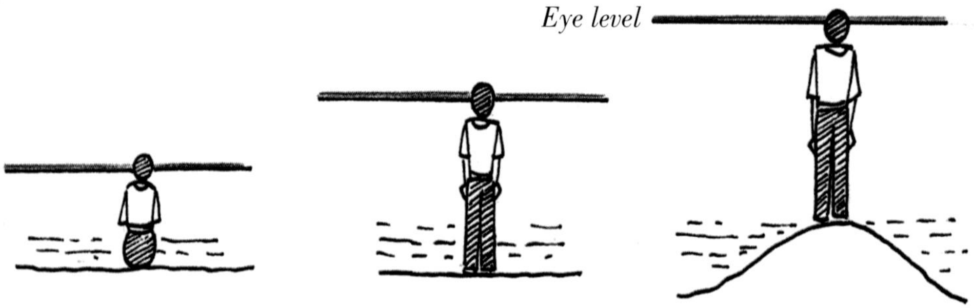

The eye level is an imaginary line, horizontally across your field of vision when you look straight ahead; not up, nor down, but straight ahead. In my sketch, I show a figure sitting low down, as if on a beach, then standing, then standing on a sand dune (*fig. 1*). Note how the eye level is always directly ahead of the figure. When looking at a real subject, look straight ahead, hold a ruler straight out with the thin edge in front of and across your eyes, and that is where your eye level is. Which comes first, the drawing in of the eyelevel or the object? Generally I suggest you draw in the object lightly first, then apply the eye level and use it with the rules of perspective to check and correct the object. One way to see perspective in action is to picture the view looking along railway lines. They appear to merge in the distance. They appear to become smaller and closer together. The point where they appear to merge is known as the *vanishing point*.

We know they do not merge in reality. I show this in my sketch (*fig. 2*). I also show the railway lines with telegraph poles on the left, then with three trees on the right. The telegraph poles and the trees in a drawing or painting would also appear to become smaller and closer together as they recede. I have shown the guidelines for each item, illustrating how the guidelines meet at the vanishing point

fig. 2

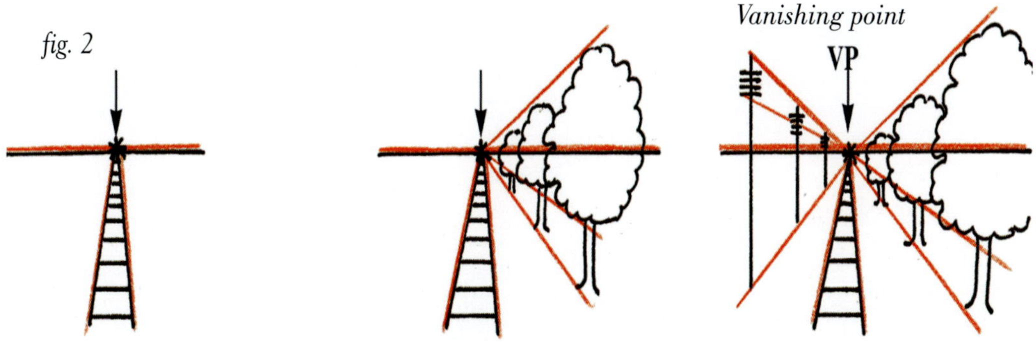

Next I show a front view of a television (*fig.3*). With this view, we have just one vanishing point for the sides of the television and for the baselines of the legs. I am imagining that you, or I, would be sitting on a normal chair of a standard height when drawing this television, in which case, I think you would find your eye level would be just about 18" above the back of the television.

In my next sketch, the television is set at an angle. Now we have two vanishing points, one for each side of it. Often guidelines want to converge on the eye level, but off the page (*fig. 4*). This is normal, and often happens. When it does, lay scrap paper at the side, tape it on from behind, and extend the guidelines onto it. Never guess or assume the perspective is correct, always try to "prove" it.

fig. 3

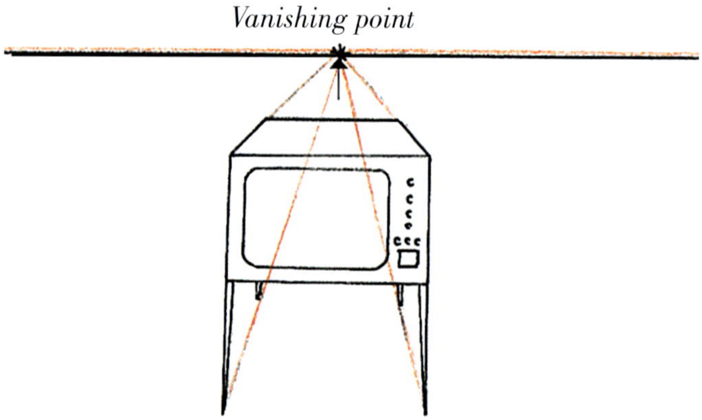

fig. 4

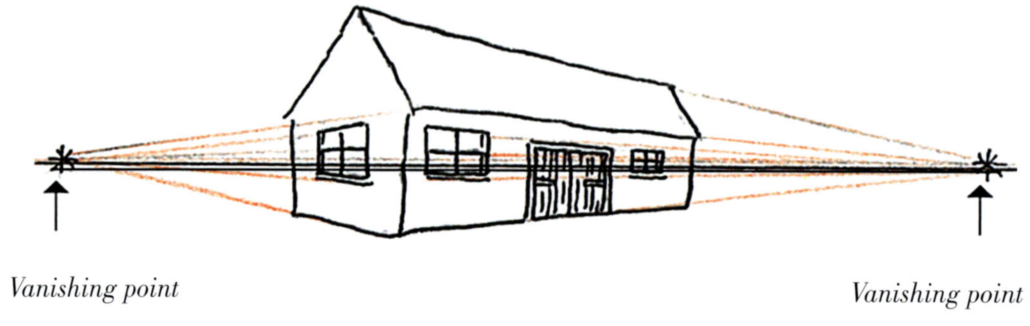

CIRCULAR PERSPECTIVE

Few people realize that perspective helps to solve the problems of drawing circles and ellipses, but it can. I have illustrated this in a sketch of three saucepans with one on its side (*fig.* 5). I have lightly drawn the group out and have placed my eye level well above it. I have then drawn a light guiding square around each ellipse we can see and have drawn those squares "in perspective," in the same way as the television. The squares for the ellipses each have their respective vanishing points on the common eye level. The two upright pans share the same vanishing point as their ellipses are on the same plane. The ellipses for the pan on its side are on a different plane so, have their own vanishing point at a different position on the eye level. The use of the squares helps determine where each vanishing point should be, to ensure the true perspective of the subject where there is an ellipse involved. I then go back to each ellipse and check that it touches the center of each side of the square it occupies, for, provided it does, I know the ellipse must be in perspective. Gently rub out the squares used outside of each ellipse and the perspective guidelines before a picture is shaded in or painted.

fig. 5

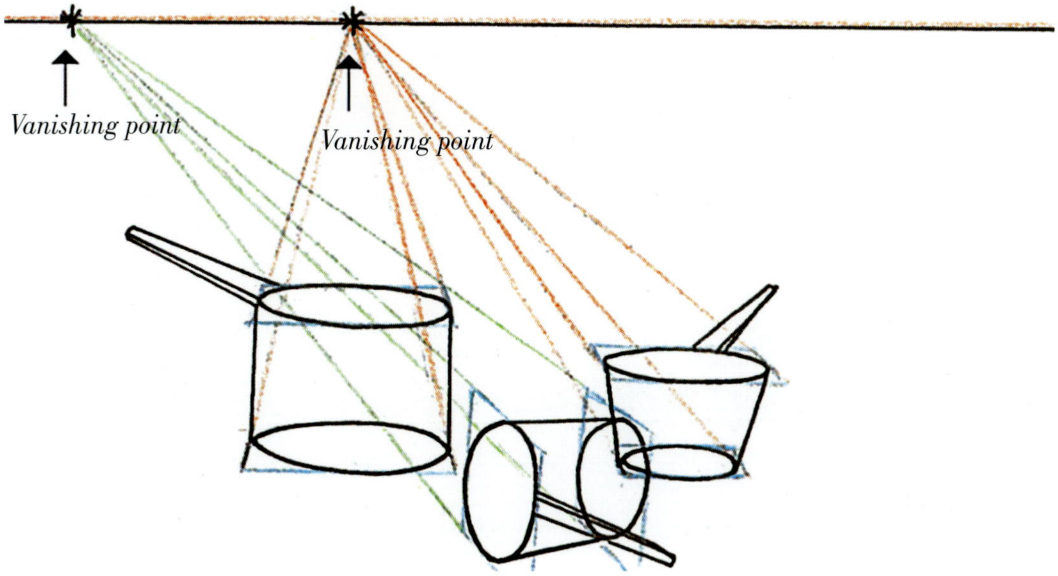

Above all else, painting should be fun. While most people wish to learn to paint pictures in the traditional manner, others like to experiment and explore other ways of expressing ideas in paint. I painted the clown for a young child. It gave the youngster a colorful picture to hang in her bedroom and it was fun to paint.

Pictures that have no easily identifiable subject, or paintings exploring abstract ideas, can be confusing to many people. They can, however, provide ways for an artist to try to convey thoughts and abstract concepts in paint. Play with the following three abstract picture techniques.

1. Take a line for a walk. Draw a long line crossing it on the painting surface, and mix and use different colors of paint to fill in each segment. When dry, outline with a fine black line if you wish.

2. Hard Edge. Try drawing simple geometric forms and painting them in colors that appeal to you.

3. Action Painting. Create an inky consistency of yellow, using turpentine and oil paint, on an old saucer. Pour blobs of the liquid yellow oil color onto your painting surface. Tip the painting up vertically and tip it from side to side so the color runs around. Let it dry. Repeat with red and let it dry. Repeat with blue.

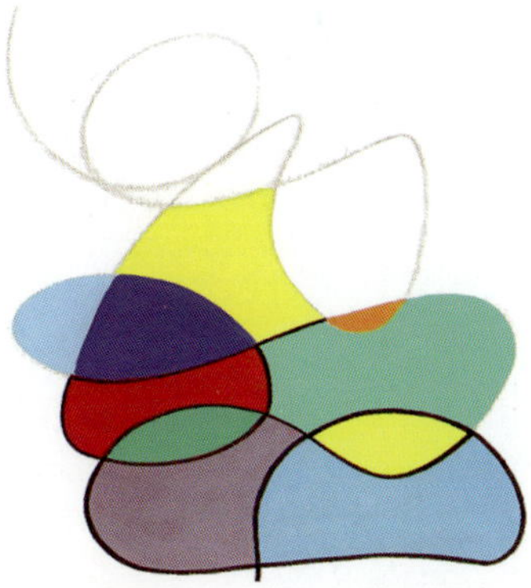

Abstract Color

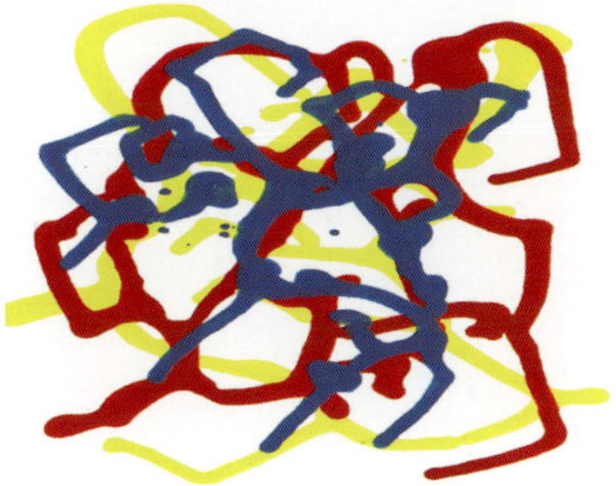

Abstract Action

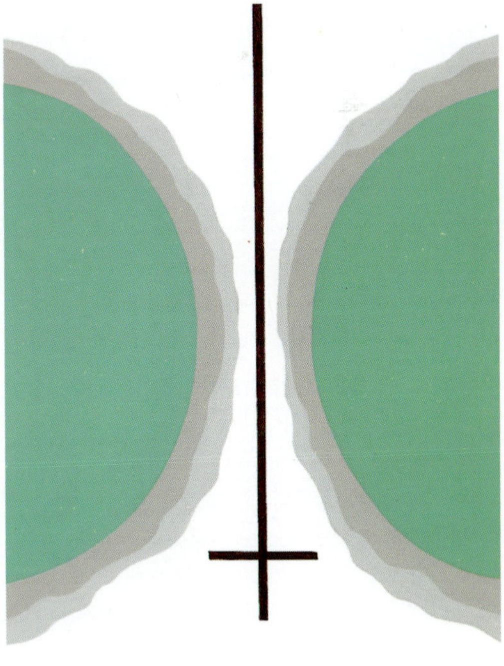

Abstract Hard Edge

OILBAR

Oilbar is an innovative and exciting dimension in artists' oil colors. Developed by artists for artists, oilbar opens up a new opportunity for picture-making and artistic expression. There is a range of thirty-five colors in three sizes known as stump, original and slim. The freedom to work directly onto the painting surface, in the same way as with charcoal or pastel, opens up all sorts of possibilities.

The colors can be applied directly to the surface of your painting support. They can be used to draw with, and one color can be rubbed with another to create blended colored effects. The sharp point of a craft knife blade or a pointed or chisel-edged piece of wood can scratch through one color to the color beneath for a wide range of effects. They can blend with a brush using a little linseed oil to achieve other effects. They are quite simply as versatile as your imagination.

When asked for ideas for your birthday present or special occasion present, this is the ideal opportunity to ask for a set of oilbars. Try out the effects described above and shown in the right-hand panel on this page.

1. Sketch the zebra with charcoal. Use black and white oilbar to fill in the stripes, blending the white stripes with gray as they come round and down the Zebra, into shadow.

2. The background scrubland and distant greens are a blend of yellow ochre, burnt umber, oxide of chromium and white. The sky is a blend of cerulean blue and white.

Oilbar marks and effects

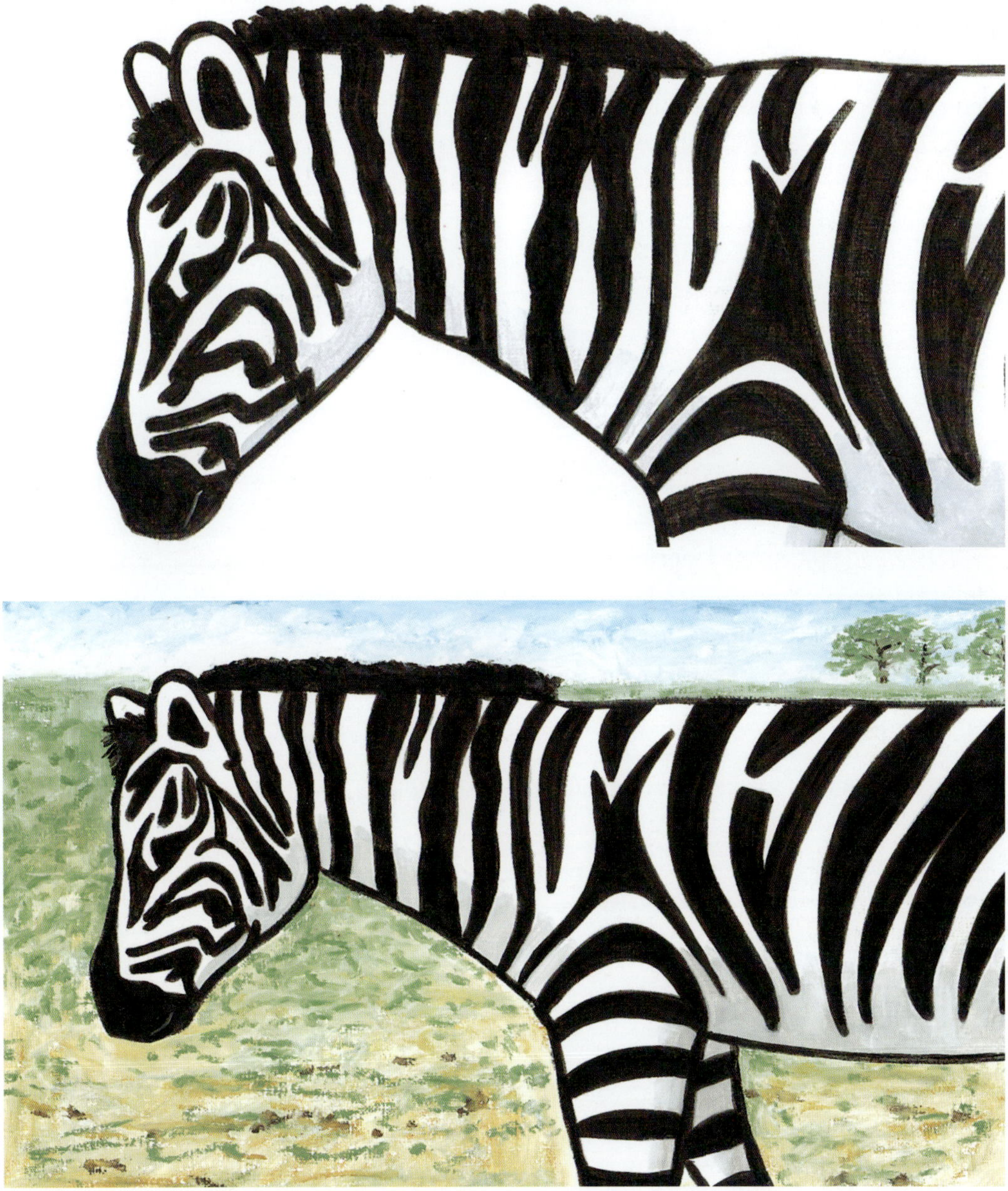

Stages in oilbar painting

PALETTE KNIVES

The palette knife is a long, straight, finger-like metal blade fixed into a wooden handle. The metal is a little thicker than for the painting knives. The palette knife essentially mixes oil paint on your palette. Plastic palette knives are also obtainable. Palette knives can apply paint to the canvas, and be used for painting as well.

The painting knives come in a wide range of shapes and have a cranked handle. This helps ensure your fingers do not touch the painted surface when applying the paint. The metal for the blade is thinner. A wide range of different marks can be produced by changing the pressure you apply to the painting knife. When selecting your first painting knife, I would recommend a medium, versatile, trowel-shaped knife.

The oil paints usually come directly from the tube and can be mixed together on the palette with no medium added. If the paint is too stiff, a little linseed oil or liquin can be mixed into the paint. If the tube paint is too runny, squeeze it onto some blotting paper for an hour or so. This will allow the surplus oil to escape from the oil paint before you transfer it to the palette.

Be generous with the amount of paint you use. You want to achieve a good texture to the paint layer. Impasto refers to this textured look. While palette knife paintings use lots of paint, it is better to paint one or two subjects with plenty of paint than several by trying to economize with the paint. Apply the paint to the picture surface and create shapes and texture marks in the wet paint with the knife. Do not allow any area you are working on to dry and then add more paint on top of that with a knife. It is rather like trying to ride a bike on a bumpy road. Work into the existing wet paint if adding other colors or effects.

Experiment using the tip, half and full blade, and the edge of your painting knife to see how many different effects and marks you can make.

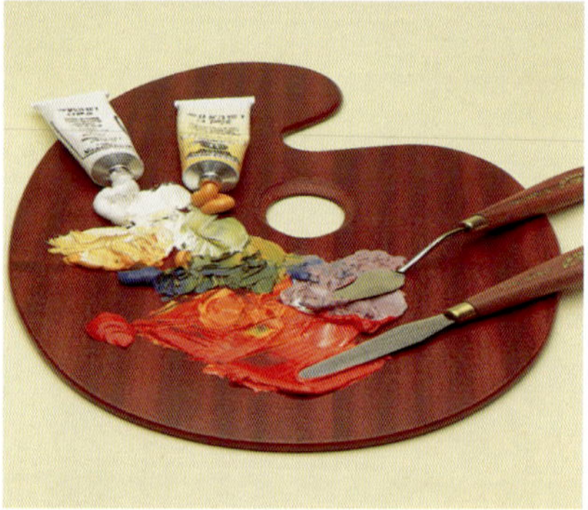

Palattes and paint

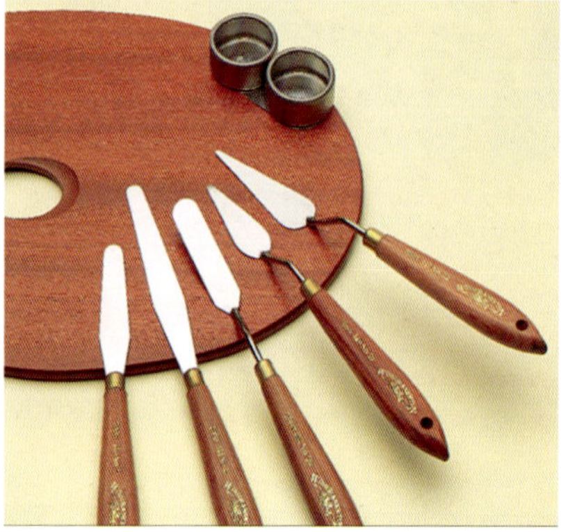

Palatte knives in different sizes

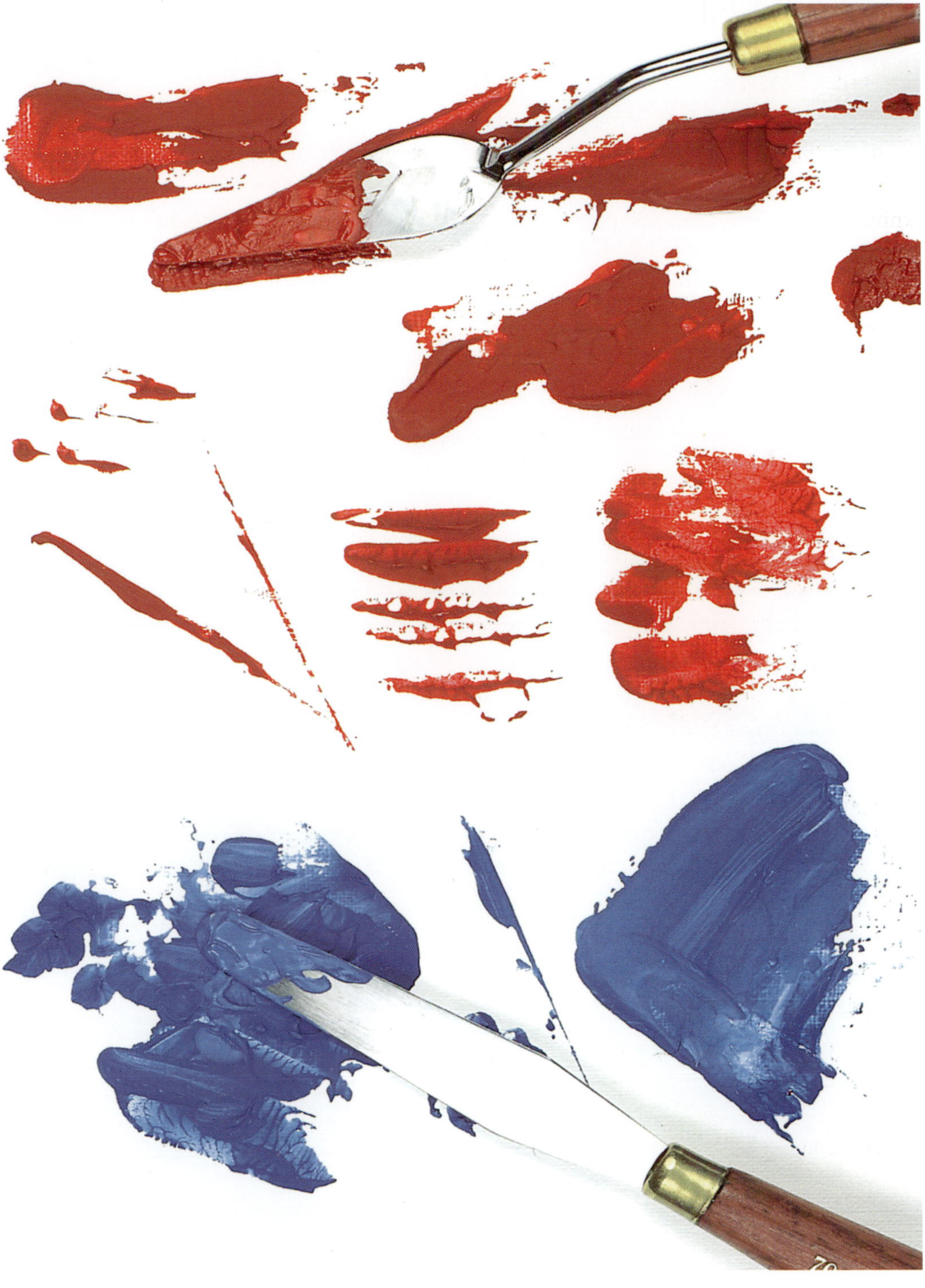

I designed this dramatic subject to help you twist and turn the wrist of your painting hand and to use a variety of painting knife marks to arrive at the finished painting. Once acquired, the knife technique works on other subjects.

1. While you should normally draw your subject prior to painting, on this occasion try the demonstration without drawing it out. Squeeze out onto your palette a generous amount of white, cadmium yellow, alizarin crimson, french ultramarine and burnt umber. Load the end of the painting knife with white and make a small circular shape for the sun. Mix white and yellow together. With a well-loaded knife, make wide knife marks of yellow, as if radiating out from the sun, as shown. Let the yellow become deeper at the outer edges.

2. Mix red, yellow and white together to make orange. Apply this, with the alizarin crimson added later, to the outer areas, spreading from yellow to orange into alizarin crimson.

3. Add the reflected sunset in the lake in exactly the same way.

4. Mix a light tone of reddish-mauve using alizarin crimson, french ultramarine and white for the silhouetted clouds and for the distant hills. Mix a medium tone of the same color for the farther hills and a darker tone for the nearest hills. Increase the amount of red and blue in the paint mixture to achieve the darker hill tones. Now repeat this for the hill reflections in the lake.

5. Make a very dark mix of deep mauve-brown from burnt umber, french ultramarine and alizarin crimson. Load the knife with the darker color and work with the thin edge of the knife turned to the surface of the picture. This should enable you to twist and turn the knife to place the medium and thin lines for the tree, fence and foreground grasses. Clean the knife and load a little bright yellowish-orange on the side and tip of the knife. Touch on the sunlit highlights to the tree trunk and branches. Add the three birds and your painting knife picture should be finished.

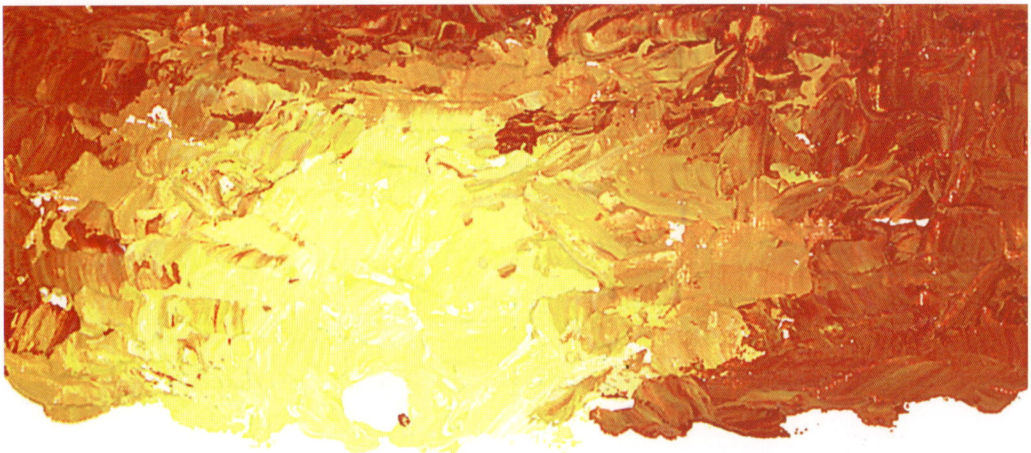

Stages 1 and 2, building with layers

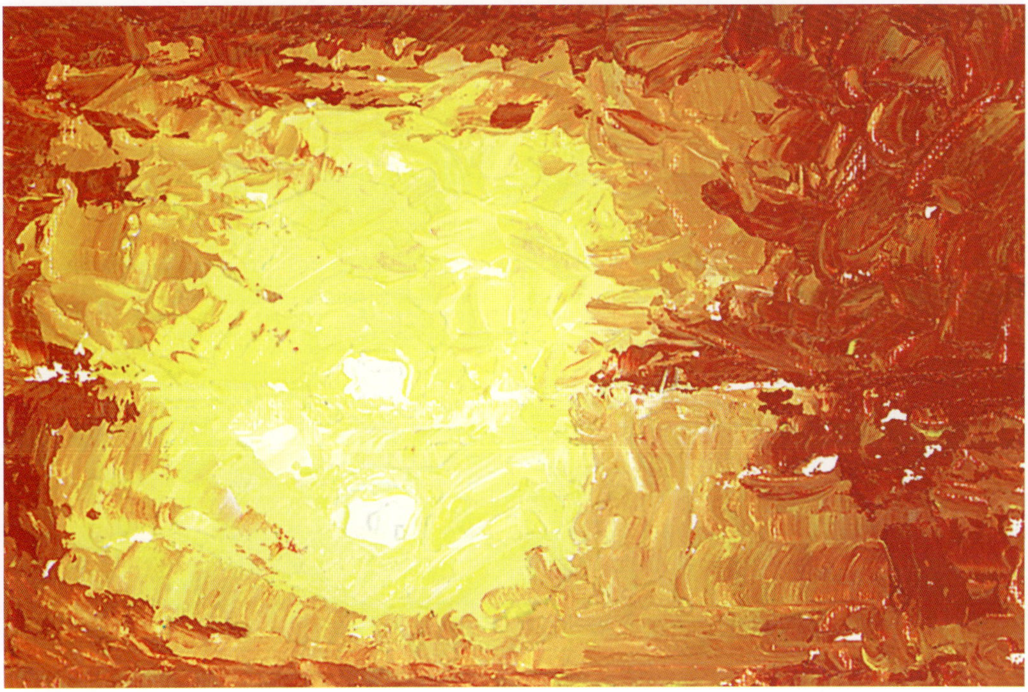

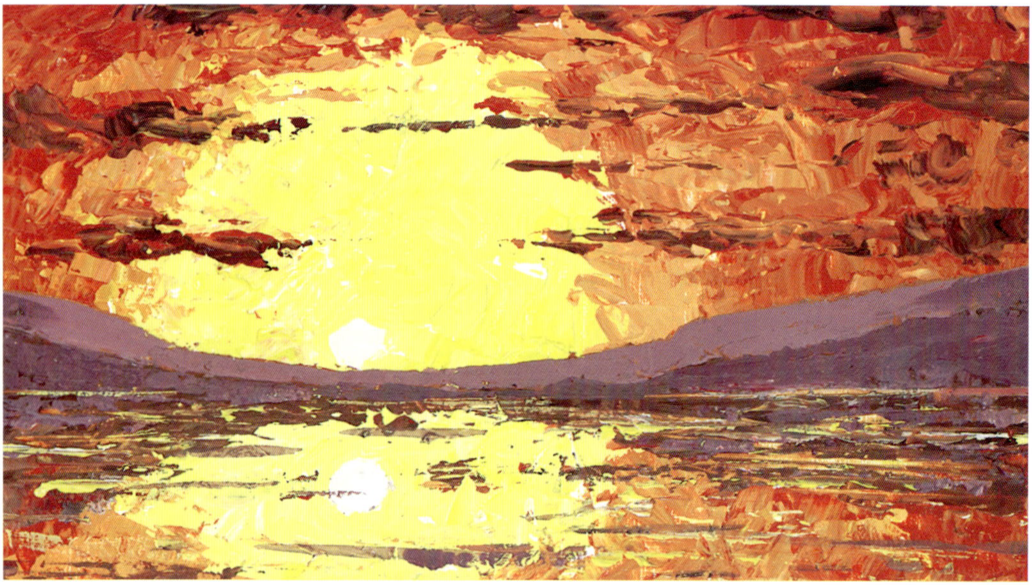

3. More paint for contrast and color

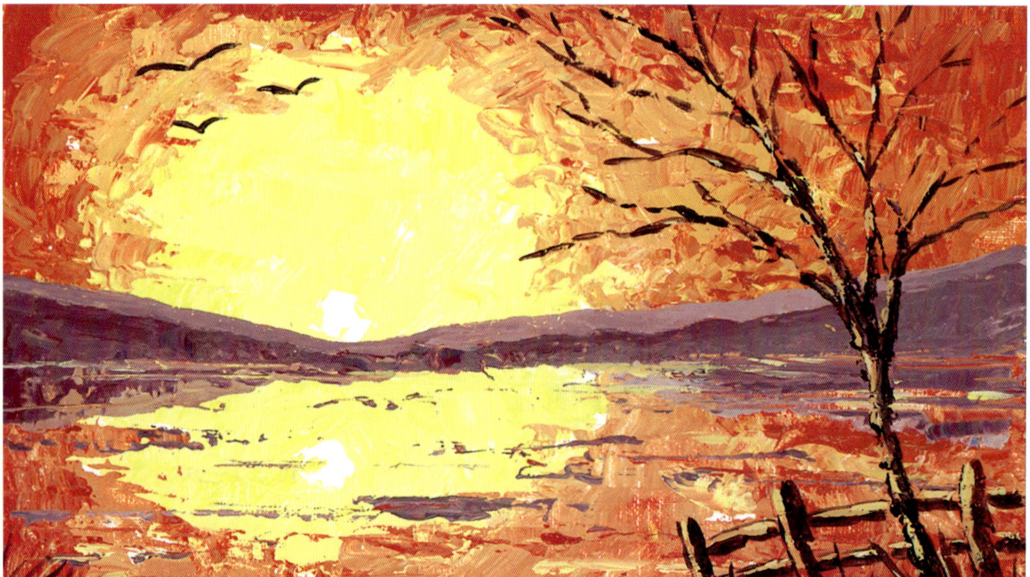

4. A finished painting with detail

GRIFFIN ALKYD PAINTS

Griffin Alkyd paints are perhaps one of the least well known of paints available to the artist. Although they have been on the market for several years, many artists are still unaware of their excellent properties and advantages. Not to be confused with the water-based acrylic paints, Alkyd paints are pigment bound in a synthetic, alkyd resin base. They behave just like oil paints but with one major advantage. The paint is normally touch-dry in around 18 hours. Liquin, the alkyd resin I have referred to in earlier chapters of this book, mixes with Alkyd paint. If you like to paint over areas of your painting, use glazing and scumbling effects, or if you like oil painting on holiday, this is a splendid paint for you. It enables you to work on the dry surface next day, instead of in several days' time. It also means that you do not have to struggle home with wet, sticky paintings from a painting holiday. I painted the picture of the Island Fort at Marmaris, Turkey, using alkyd paints. The colors are stable and light fast, and the paint rigorously tested by the manufacturers.

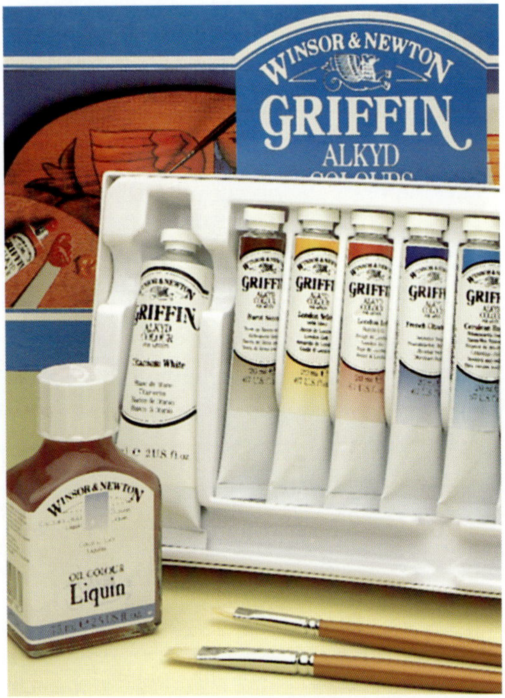

Griffin Alkyd paints

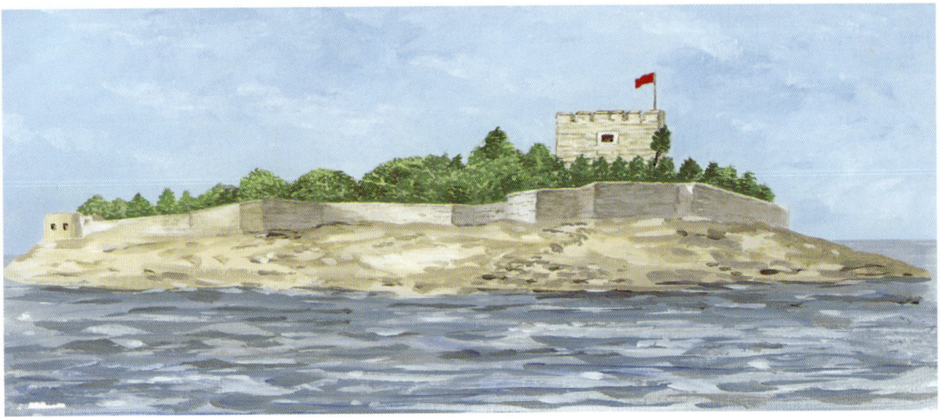

An example of an alkyd painting

GLAZING AND SCUMBLING

If you are familiar with watercolor painting, you will know how one translucent layer is laid on top of another, which helps achieve some of the characteristic effects of that medium. Thin, translucent layers of oil color can be brushed over a previously dry layer of oil paint. The thin wash tints the painted area underneath. Make the thin mix of color by mixing extra linseed oil and turpentine to the oil color to be used for tinting.

Glaze is the term for applying a light tint over a darker color. The term scumble describes a dark tint over a light color. As the oil/turpentine mix can take several days to dry before other tints or work can be carried out, it can be a lengthy process to arrive at the finished effect. If you make the color tint using liquin, it can be applied over dry oil paint and the tint is touch-dry next day. If you use Griffin Alkyd paints for the whole picture, the opaque paint layers and the glazes and scumbles will all be touch-dry around 18 hours after they are applied. For those artists who like to add glazes and scumbles this is a major advantage. Familiarize yourself with the properties of glazes and scumbles:

1. Paint three long brush strokes—red, yellow and blue. Leave a space between them. Let the paint dry. Mix each color with liquin on your palette. Apply three more brush strokes using the translucent red, blue and yellow at right angles as shown. Let them dry. Note the effect of the glazes and scumbles.

2. Paint the piece of wood illustrated using burnt umber, french ultramarine and white. Let it dry. Mix a thin glaze of burnt sienna and liquin. Brush the translucent color on top of the left-hand half of the wood. When it is dry, compare the two halves.

3. Paint a tonal gray apple. Let it dry. Apply a thin glaze of yellow. Let it dry. Apply a thin scumble of green, leaving part of the left side the original yellow. Let it dry. Apply a thin scumble of darker green on the right side. Let it dry. Add the shadow to the apple casts. Create the apple with glazes and scumbles on a gray background.

With practice and imagination, you will find situations when painting in oils where you can use glazes and scumbles to good effect.

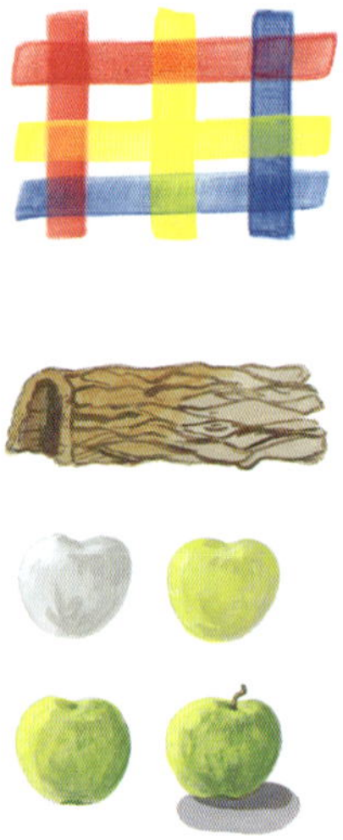

Three examples of glazes and scumbles

VARNISHING AND FRAMING OIL PAINTINGS

Allow at least six months for your painting to become thoroughly dry. During this period, it will appear to lose some of the richness and sheen of the fresh oil paint. Varnishing the picture will help regain this effect. Oil paintings are normally free from framing under glass, so the varnish also acts to protect the surface of the painting from the atmosphere. You can apply either a gloss varnish or a matte varnish depending on your preference. The gloss varnish brings back the richness of the original colors. Gloss varnish comes in bottles. Lay the picture down on a newspaper-covered table. Pour the bottle varnish into a clean dish and, using a large, flat, clean bristle brush apply the varnish from top to bottom. The picture should remain flat while the varnish dries.

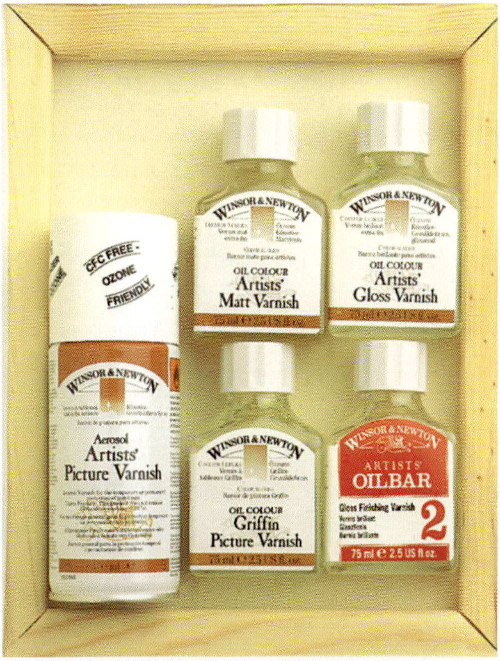

Examples of Varnish

Alternatively, you can spray the picture with an aerosol of picture varnish. Spray a light coat left to right, top to bottom, and the next day spray a second coat, but at right angles to the first coat. You can often buy frames ready-made, or made to fit. The choice of a picture frame is personal. It depends on what feel looks right with your picture, or where it is going to hang. A good local framer will often offer the benefit of his experience and show you a selection of moldings that might work for the painting. For artists who like to make their own frames, suitable moldings sell in art supply stores.

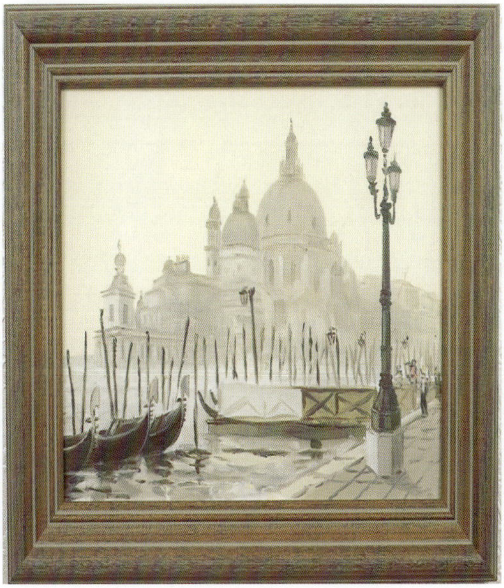

A finished, framed painting

EXHIBITING AND SELLING YOUR WORK

Most people like to keep their first paintings or give them to family or friends. As the standard of your work develops, start to consider the opportunities to exhibit and sell some of that work. I would certainly recommend considering joining a local arts club or society. Art galleries and libraries usually have details for such groups. You will often find that helpful support, friendship, visiting artists demonstrating their techniques, and the opportunity to show work will all become available to you. Galleries and libraries usually have details of forthcoming local, regional and national exhibitions. Exhibitions can vary from pictures hung on street railings, to work hung on the walls of a famous gallery. Local stores, restaurants and building societies often take and display art on a sale-or-return basis.

It is customary to offer a percentage of such a sale to that establishment. Most towns and cities have open exhibitions where artists in the vicinity submit work. As more work often enters than there is space to hang it, a selection committee often chooses work. Acceptance is an exhilarating feeling. Many people find rejection dispiriting. Good work often finds rejection due to the lack of space. It may be that they already have a similar painting. Work rejected by one exhibit often finds acceptance at another.

You can always mark your paintings NFS, or Not for Sale, if you want to display but do not want to sell them. If you offer work for sale but find yourself uncertain of the price to charge, a local framer or a senior member of an art gallery will have knowledge of current prices.

Keep copies of the receipts for art materials and frames that you buy, any expense you incur, and the sales that you make, in case you find your income from such sales as taxable. Copyright is the infringement of an artist's exclusive right to determine the copy of their work. It holds for the period of seventy to one hundred years after the artist's death. Many artists, especially art tutors and artist/authors like me, have no objection to students copying paintings as a means of learning the art of painting.

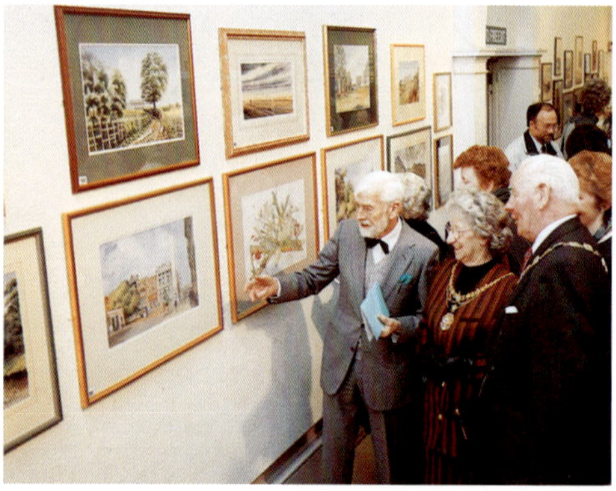

PICTURE SHAPES

Experiment. Most painting supports come in rectangular form. Many artists just paint their pictures, filling the traditional shape. It is possible to buy other shapes of canvass and frames. These can make for exiting picture compositions and are very welcome at art exhibitions.

Horizontal rectangle

Vertical rectangle

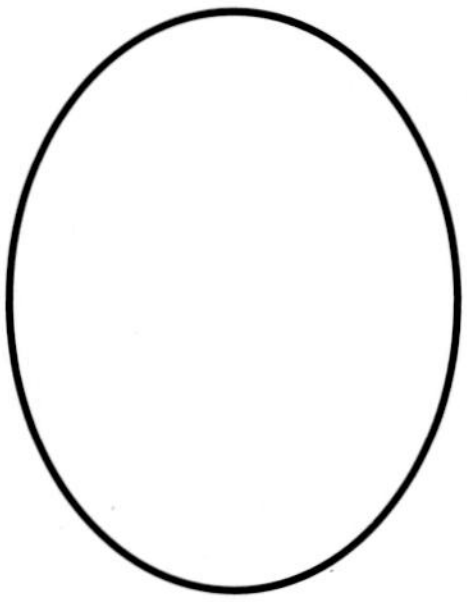

Oval

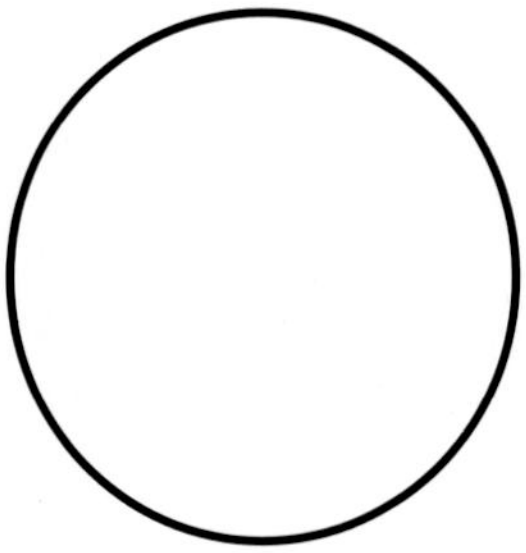

Circular

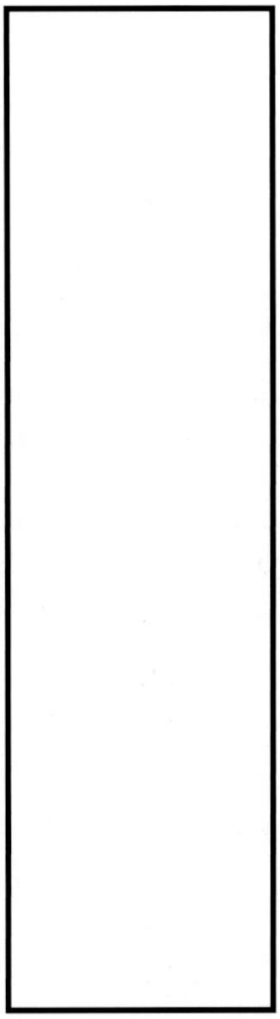

Tall thin rectangle

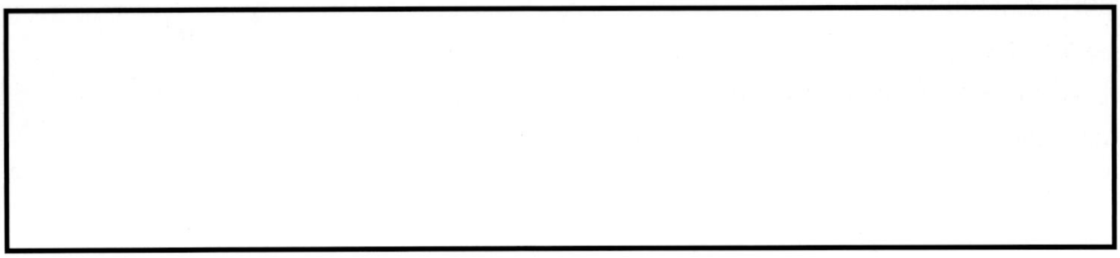

Long thin rectangle

SOME HELPFUL DO'S AND DON'TS

- Do copy out the color charts on pages 14 and 15 and keep them by you when painting.
- Do try out the different methods for sketching your subject described in Demonstration 1.
- Do wear old clothes or an overall when oil painting.
- Do experiment with your brushes to see the different types of marks and effects each brush shape can achieve.
- Do try out the Alla Prima (wet on wet) technique and also the methods which allow each stage to dry.
- Don't forget to turn your sketch upside down to check its accuracy before you paint it.
- Don't forget to try out palette knife painting.
- Don't forget that some of the best subjects are to be found in everyday objects and everyday situations.
- Don't forget to look for, and show, the light, medium and dark tones in your subject and to emphasize the very lightest and the very darkest features in your painting.
- Don't forget to ENJOY your painting.

Remember, if you have ever said "I wish I could paint,"
my message to you is...

IF YOU WANT TO…YOU CAN